Experiencing Social Work

Experiencing Social Work

Learning from Service Users

Mark Doel and Lesley Best

Los Angeles • London • New Delhi • Singapore

SAGE Publications Ltd
1 Oliver's Yard
55 City Road
London EC1Y 1SP

SAGE Publications Inc.
2455 Teller Road
Thousand Oaks, California 91320

SAGE Publications India Pvt Ltd
B 1/I 1 Mohan Cooperative Industrial Area
Mathura Road
New Delhi 110 044

SAGE Publications Asia-Pacific Pte Ltd
33 Pekin Street #02-01
Far East Square
Singapore 048763

Library of Congress Control Number: 2007932605

British Library Cataloguing in Publication data

A catalogue record for this book is available from the
British Library

ISBN 978-1-4129-1021-7
ISBN 978-1-4129-1022-4 (pbk)

Typeset by CEPHA Imaging Pvt. Ltd., Bangalore, India
Printed and bound in Great Britain by TJ International Ltd,
Padstow, Cornwall
Printed on paper from sustainable resources

To the memory of Mary Thomson

Contents

Preface

Why this book?

The social work library has grown enormously over the past few decades. From a slim 'Library of Social Work' series in the early 1970s, most major publishing houses now have a large social work list, with book series and journals, too. Whether the focus is theory or skills, the legal framework or the social context, there is an extensive choice of literature. Not quite so well documented, however, are the specifics of the practice of social work. What do social workers actually do and how do they do it? Even rarer are accounts of how social work is experienced. As a relatively private encounter between two or more people, we have limited access to social work, and the accounts that are available are often mediated by academic researchers and aggregated into statistical rather than particular experiences. The combined picture of social work from all these sources, though valuable, is out of balance.

Some other perspectives are available. For example, practitioners' recordings in case files and portfolios of practice are sometimes seen as part of the 'grey' literature. However, these are rarely incorporated into academic referencing and because it is this latter evidence base which gives rise to most of the explicit theorising about social work, the voice of practitioners remains relatively weak.

Least heard are the voices of the people who experience social work directly, either as users of the services or as the carers of these people. There is evidence of increased service user and carer involvement in services (Carr, 2004) and the value of service user organisations informing future welfare policy (Beresford and Turner, 1997; Blueprint Project, 2004; Shaping Our Lives[1]); however, accounts of the direct experiences of service users and carers remain unusual (Cree and Davis, 2007; Heriot and Polinger, 2002).

In the light of this, we have two imperatives. The one is to give greater voice to those who directly experience social work. By listening to the perspectives of these people, we challenge the nature of the knowledge that drives social work as an activity. We challenge the explanations about behaviours and beliefs that are so often steered by professional research and theorising, for we must not assume that the understandings of professionals and service users coincide (Napier and Fook, 2000).

[1] www.shapingourlives.org.uk.

The incorporation of service users' accounts as equal partners in the pursuit of knowledge is a search for meaningful understanding rather than scientific explanation, and an acknowledgement that 'dependable scientific knowledge may well prove elusive' (Taylor and White, 2000: 5.) It is an opportunity for the people who are too often the subjects of practice to provide a critique of that practice and for all of us to incorporate the learning from these critiques into our own practice. So, if the first imperative is to give voice to develop a better understanding of meaning, the second is to find ways in which these voices can be integrated into the more formal literature and to contribute to our theorising about social work.

Recounting positive experiences

Another factor which unbalances the picture of social work is the tendency to focus on social work when it fails. True, some proponents of social work have contributed to this by pathologising clients and focusing on ideas of inadequacy and dysfunction. Thankfully, there are methods of practice which redress this balance by harnessing people's capabilities (Marsh and Doel, 2005; Pichot and Dolan, 2003), but the reality of practice can too often fall short of the rhetoric of the strengths model. This focus on what is wrong is reinforced by media that are searching for and selecting bad news and are often ideologically hostile to social work. The relative absence of a social work voice in the face of a hostile press is further highlighted by regular public inquiries into the tragic consequences of poor and dangerous practices. No doubt socio-biologists can explain why there seems to be something hard-wired about the human propensity to select what is worng. We can safely assume, for example, that you focused on the word that was spelled wrongly in the previous sentence and not the twenty that were correct.

There is a political imperative to assert social work as a positive force in post-industrial society, like groupwork's active role in democratising post-war Germany (Kalcher, 2004). Social work *is* a political activity, not just in terms of the power dynamics between the people involved, but as an expression of individual and collective care and responsibility and a passionate commitment to social justice and empowerment for those beyond the pale of mainstream society. Social work operates in a political context which is competitive and reactive, and it is essential that we find ways to promote it, even 'brand' it. All of this is necessary if we are to build broad public support for what social work is and what it stands for. It is a civilising force.

We need to celebrate the successes of social work. This is especially important when we consider the depth of public ignorance about what social work is. Judged by its limited portrayal in the lives of soap operas, this unawareness is enormous. All professions tend to be portrayed stereotypically, but many, such as nursing, teaching and the police, are represented through a broad range of stereotypes. Social work is comparatively restricted; either the woolly–minded, easily conned, ineffective sandal-wearer or the hard-as-nails, officious, dawn-raid harridan. The need for active promotion to promote public understanding of social work is urgent. A rather subtle UK government campaign to recruit social workers using story-line cartoons was one step in this direction, though a small one. Accounts of the direct encounters that people have with social work could be a powerful way of making the case.

When people tell their own story they have control of the way it is constructed. However, we need also to be aware that all narratives have a choreography that is influenced by the particular audience (Taylor, 2006). Practitioners might present positive pictures of their practice in their portfolios in order to influence the assessment of their work, though they can still be a showcase for authentic positive practices (Doel et al., 2002; Smith, 2003) and an important alternative to the prescription of the textbook or the denunciation of the public inquiry. Readers will come to their own conclusion about the authenticity of the stories in this book; suffice it to say that those who contributed gave them openly and enthusiastically.

Relationships and contexts

When we ask people about their positive experiences of social work, we find that they are more likely to be concerned with the virtues of their particular social worker – their honesty, trustworthiness and intelligence – rather than whether they comply with an abstract ethical code or a set of moral standards. This 'virtue ethics' (Clark, 2006) places individual practitioners firmly centre-stage, in terms of their character rather than their role (Marquis and Jackson, 2000; Saarnio, 2000).

These personal characteristics are interconnected; for example, trust is linked with a shared understanding of confidentiality, and helping people to understand the limits to confidentiality is one way in which the delicateness of trust can be maintained (Swain, 2006). We will see that the relationship with the social worker is central to the narratives in this book. Not a surprising finding, but one that needs continual reinforcement, as bullet-pointed procedures spread like bindweed across professional practice. By listening to people's encounters with social work we might be able to arrive at a more person-centred definition of practice (Gambrill, 2003).

What research we have reinforces the picture revealed by the stories in this book, that the quality of the relationship between workers and service users is important (Bland et al., 2006; Lee and Ayon, 2004). Children in care tell us that they want to keep a relationship going with a social worker or care worker even when they move placement because 'good relationships with professionals are squandered' (Voice for the Child in Care, 2004). They also emphasize the significance of friendship groups that pre-date their transition into care and that they want more opportunities to keep in touch with them. These ideas challenge current practices, though they are what *we* would want if we were in that position.

Do the stories in this book merely tell us that a positive experience of social work is just about being a nice, reliable person? Of course not. We will learn that these encounters also reveal the fascinating complexity of social work, not just in terms of understanding human experience, but in helping to shape it alongside changing contexts – political, social, legal, professional and organisational. These stories reveal social work as an applied social science, a practical moral philosophy and a committed social activism, all combined.

'Social work has always been, first and foremost, an enterprise imbued with moral purpose and values and not merely a technical expertise' (Clark, 2006: 77). What is unusual, perhaps unique, about social work is that its concern extends to people's lives *as a whole*. This is why the move to specialisms has been so injurious to social work's mission because it conflicts with the core value that has a holistic view of people's lives. Where organisations see discrete categories of 'mental health', 'children' and 'older adults', social work sees *people* in families and communities – in fact, much as people see themselves.

It is some years now since *The Client Speaks* (Mayer and Timms, 1970) burst on the social work scene. How radical – a book that actually reported what clients thought about their encounters with social workers; and the shock that these perceptions frequently differed from the workers' perspectives. This tradition was strengthened by later works, such as Sainsbury (1989) and Rees (1978), who researched what people valued about social workers, and then what they wanted from them (Harding and Beresford, 1996). Other studies have thrown light on what other professionals value about social work (Herod and Lymbery, 2002).

Finding out what people think about their services is now no longer a novelty. Indeed, the growth of satisfaction surveys is in danger of leading to research fatigue amongst 'consumers' who might rightly wonder what differences their opinions make to the actual service. The usefulness of these surveys has been called into question, especially since they offer such a passive form of involvement (Crawford and Kessel, 1999; Walsh and Lord, 2003). So, it is one thing to ask someone 'How was it for you?' and another to invite them to tell their story, to listen actively, to act on it and to learn from it.

The book makes no claim to tell the full story. There are missing elements. For example, we learn something about 'the everyday, routine processes by which social work is accomplished' (Taylor, 2006: 190), but the methods used by the practitioners to accomplish their work can only be inferred from the service users' descriptions. We need more accounts from practitioners themselves (Cree and Davis, 2007; Doel, 2006; Marsh and Doel, 2005).

Service users and practitioners know by experience that much of the subtlety of practice is missed by the kinds of indicator and target that are imposed by those who do not take part in these encounters. 'Social workers display considerable skill in monitoring potential risks whilst engaging with families, and the subtleties involved in such activity are not captured by official measures of governance which concentrate on more abstract indicators of performance' (Spratt and Callan, 2004: 199). We hope that the conversations in this book can reveal some of this subtlety.

Acknowledgements

We are grateful to all the people who gave their stories for this book; specifically to Enable Housing Association in Chesterfield for facilitating our contacts with the people who told their stories in Chapter 9, to Diane Gower and Maplefields School in Corby (Chapter 10) and to Paul Carr and the Northamptonshire Early Intervention in Psychosis Service (Chapter 8).

Our thanks to all those who helped to put us in touch with people who contributed to this book, in particular SCIE's Partners Council. We would also like to thank Zoe Elliott-Fawcett and Anna Luker at SAGE for their gentle encouragement.

1 Introduction

'I have to be frank, when I volunteered my story I was sceptical about what difference telling it could make. But now I am convinced'

This book aims to provide some small rebalancing. There are two ways we hope to achieve this. First, by providing accounts of social work from the point of view of the people who directly experience it. Practitioners do, at least, have portfolios to collect narratives of their experiences, but the people currently styled service users or self-advocates do not have this means of expression.

A second aspect of this rebalancing is the decision to collect narratives of *positive* experiences of social work. Direct accounts of people's experience of social work are unusual enough, narratives of positive experience are rarer still. We want to counter the public inquiry phenomenon; whoever heard of a public inquiry into what went spectacularly right? So, this book is based on the premise that we can learn as much, perhaps more, from what goes right as what goes wrong. Although it can be useful to learn from experiences that fall all too short of good practice (Malone et al., 2005), we believe that there is not a good balance, with students exposed to few if any specific examples of good practice. The recounting of a single example can have a powerful impact, as with Hingley-Jones' (2005) exploration of the emotional component of the parent – professional relationship with a child with autistic spectrum disorder. Lists of bullet-pointed principles of practice have their limitations, and exhortations to good practice in social work texts are not enough.

Of course, this book cannot claim to be representative in any way, since we do not know the prevalence of these kinds of positive experience of social work. However, we know through our own and others' direct experiences that the pictures presented in the public media and the professional literature neglect one of the realities; there is much unsung good practice.

Whilst acknowledging the importance of formal research into social work outcomes and aggregated statistical evidence, we hope this book can play its part in contributing to the knowledge base. Although our role has been as much journalist as social researcher, we have been aware of our particular responsibilities as narrators in some of this process and have aimed to be accurate and respectful. The process of finding and recording these narratives is detailed later in the chapter.

Speaking up for social work

This book is an attempt to articulate the process of social work through an alliance of service user and professional, in telling social work stories and reflecting on them. Beresford and Croft (2004) are right that social work is unlikely to develop a more emancipatory role until social workers play a central role in its construction and gain support for that role by developing much closer partnerships and collaborations with service users and their organizations and movements. So, the book is a forum for service users and self-advocates to reflect on their encounters with social work and for practitioners and students to learn from these reflections. It is in the tradition of story-telling, similar to Lecroy's (2002) account of what makes up the 'dailyness' of the lives of social workers. Our book is less about the dailyness of service users' experience and more a gathering of their thoughts about the entirety of their encounter. For those listening to these stories, it becomes evident that what social workers do is at once simple and complex.

Social work is, rightly, a largely private affair, but with the consequence that it is largely invisible (Pithouse, 1998). This privacy prevents scrutiny and hides the learning and celebration that could be gained from wider knowledge of the positive benefits of social work. It also contrasts with the glare of publicity that surrounds those examples of social work that has gone terribly wrong. If we might move from sight to sound in this metaphor, the noise of bad practices is a cacophony that drowns the tranquillity of good practices and it prevents us from knowing what the true balance is between the two. You cannot measure the 'amount' of quiet behind the roar. So, to recount some positive experiences of social work is a way to search behind the roar, whether it is social workers' narratives (Cree, 2003) or the people they work with (Cree and Davis, 2007). We hope that the reflections of the many people in this book can help to articulate what social work is; and, for the wider community, this is a window on what actually goes on when people encounter social work. For students and practitioners it sheds light on how to achieve practice that is experienced positively.

It is reasonable to ask who the contributors to this book felt were 'the audience' and how this might have affected the way they constructed their stories. Is there a 'Hawthorn effect' here, in which the positive aspects of their experience are exaggerated because that is what the story-teller knows the listener is expecting? We cannot know for sure, only that the contributors selected themselves because they felt strongly that they wanted to share their experiences *because* they were largely good. The desire for inclusion led one of the self-advocates in Chapter 9 to ask to tell his experiences of social work, even though they were generally negative, but this was, uniquely, the exception.

How the book was written

The book is inspired by the desire to give voice to service users and to help practitioners and students to learn from experiences of social work that are, by and large, positive. What is clear is that even when service users are participating, such as developing and delivering social work education, it is usually via the invitation of the professionals, who largely set the agenda. An approach that seeks to challenge this is both time-consuming and unpredictable and it relies on the emergence of trust through a process where the professionals let go of power.

A parallel influence was the emerging literature on service user involvement, that revealed the tendency for professionals to appropriate service users' knowledge and reframe it as their own (Beresford and Croft, 2004). We wanted the process of telling the story, and how it was told (written by the service user or through the authors) to be empowering rather than expropriating (Johnston and Hatton, 2003). The book contains accounts written by service users themselves and others that were documented through conversation (Murphy et al., 2001). It was important that each person chose their particular method. All the contributors knew that the guiding principle was the fact that they had a generally positive story to tell in terms of their experience of social work.

Finding the stories in this book has been serendipitous. Although the plan called for a range of people across the UK, from a variety of backgrounds and in different circumstances, the reality has been more opportunistic. The process has been what researchers term 'snowballing'; we set several balls rolling and hoped they would pick up people who wanted to participate along the way. For example, SCIE's Partners Council of service users, carers and self-advocates was a very helpful starting point. For a variety of reasons, numerous leads ended in cul-de-sacs; even so, these journeys were invariably interesting and worthwhile.

Once tentative contact had been made with people who had expressed interest in telling their story, we introduced the broad purpose of the book as a way of painting a picture of social work and, by focusing on experiences that were generally positive, helping this and future generations of social workers to learn about good practice. As well as the opportunity to tell their stories, people also expressed pleasure at being able to contribute to improving experiences for future others.

In addition to discussing the purpose of the book, we made sure that people were confident that their anonymity would be protected. This confidentiality included the knowledge that what was said would not affect the services that were being received. These issues of privacy were more important to some contributors than to others, though everyone enjoyed choosing the name they would like to be known by in the book.

We had considered the ethical dimensions to this project at some length, gaining independent review and consultation. The questions that helped us to test ethical concerns focused on the motivation for writing the book and whether this format was the most effective way of meeting the objectives of the book, both of which we have discussed in this introduction and in the Preface.

We met the person wherever they suggested they would feel most comfortable and suggested options for how the story might be recounted. A big decision for each service user was whether to write the story themselves or have the authors act as journalist. Julia and Leone chose to recount their own stories, Julia by writing it herself and Leone by transposing from an audio cassette. Two young people who had experienced local authority care also decided to write their story after the conversation, but the moment passed and their story with it. The authors and the contributors signed an agreement which was clear that contributors could withdraw their story at any stage up to publication. It was acknowledged that the telling of personal stories may revisit painful life experiences and we asked participants to think about this and discussed access to personal support, should they need this.

In general we suggested a preference for making notes during our conversations rather than using tape recordings, though Leone asked for a tape so that her story could be transposed directly. This method relied on us writing up the conversation promptly and making a draft available to the person soon after, so that the conversation was still fresh in the mind. For those who could not read, supporters were primed to receive and read out the drafts. Some people were happy that the draft captured what they had said very well, others came back with suggestions for some changes, including things that had come to mind after the conversation. For example, Mrs Corbett decided she wanted to use a different name for her husband.

The arrangements for the self-advocates' chapter were different, in that both authors participated together in the group story-telling, then met separately with individuals to hear their stories. Every member of the group and their supporters had access to the draft of the group's story, whilst the privacy of individual stories was maintained.

Story and narrative

If the story is the events and the narrative is the telling of the events, then this book is about both. In describing the process of narration above, we can see that the construction of each person's story was a collaboration between the service users and the authors. The conversations were guided by a purpose, in this case to explore a generally positive experience of social work, how it had been positive and why. Perhaps the notion of *encounter* best combines the sense of the events and also the telling of them, for in the process of recounting events, the service users were also reflecting on these experiences and, to some extent, reconstructing them.

An interesting aspect of the building of the book is the fact that, though the focus of each person's story is themselves, it also centres on someone who is not in the room – the social worker (or student social worker in some cases). For the authors, it also concerned an abstract process, that of *social working* (Carter et al., 1995). At one time in the planning of the book, we considered having conversations with each of the social workers, where possible and only, of course, with the service user's permission. This would give another perspective on each of the stories. However, in writing the book, we came to feel that the social workers' stories were not necessary and could threaten to blunt the service users' accounts. Like a person in a play who is often referred to but never appears, it was felt better for the social worker to remain off-stage, someone left to the reader's imagination. In this way we can imagine the social worker in this book as a collectivity rather than a series of different individuals.

Of course, the act of recounting the social work story is a re-construction of that story. 'An understanding and analysis of narratives and the role they play in the politics of people's lives, at macro and micro levels, can be used effectively in changing the politics of situations. The process of change can be characterised quite simply as one of narrative reconstruction' (Fook, 2002: 135). Just as people's life stories can be recovered through social work itself (and life scripts challenged as a consequence), so their stories *of* social work were reconstructed through these conversations (Solas, 1995). Indeed, we could not have guessed the full potential of this process until the events recounted in the Epilogue to the final chapter (see page 134).

Children's story-telling is rather different from adults and none of the stories in this book are directly from children, though one (Leone, Chapter 6) concerns her time as a child and others (the families) report on children's experiences of their social workers. No doubt there are similarities between what adults find positive in their experience of social work and what children do, but there are likely to be important distinctions, too (Horwath, 2001). Certainly, doing research with children requires different methods of communication to enable self-expression (Fraser et al., 2004; Lancaster and Broadbent, 2003; Lewis et al., 2004; Thomas and O'Kane, 2000). For example, children's stories may best be expressed through their drawings (Coates, 2004) and we are pleased to reproduce two of these in this book (see Chapter 10). The issues and ethics of consent are also different with children, though they are increasingly seen as their own experts (Williams, 2006). There are organisations which provide a platform for children and young people's experiences (e.g. A National Voice[1]; Young Minds[2]) and some studies have documented positive experiences. The comment of one child, that social workers were 'there for you if you needed them to be' (Aubrey and Dahl, 2006: 33) is repeated by many of the adults and young people in this book.

As noted, we wished to include examples of positive experiences of social work in the widest range of settings, but the serendipitous nature of our contacts means that some settings must await a future volume. Sometimes people's circumstances changed, such as the woman who wanted to tell the story of her successful transition from home to residential care and her positive encounter with social work, but who became too ill to tell her story. By no means all the people's stories are about voluntary engagement with social work (Humerah, for example, has experienced numerous compulsory admissions to psychiatric care), and it is natural to wonder whether positive experiences of social work are more likely to be confined to contacts with service users on a voluntary, helping basis. What about the experiences where social work polices the boundaries of society, such as immigration controls (Humphries, 2004)? More of these kinds of story must also await a further volume.

What is also missing is any judgement about how commonplace these positive experiences are. There is no claim that the book is representative and there has been no attempt to sample, other than to include stories from as wide a range of people as possible. However, the face of social work that we described earlier and in the Preface (from the media, from government inquiries and even from social work texts) is not representative either. The book is inspired precisely by the desire to achieve some rebalancing; it is not intended to suggest that all or most social work is experienced in the ways recounted in this book. We cannot know how typical or unusual these kinds of encounter are.

With some exceptions (notably Julia and Leone), context is relatively absent from these stories. In focusing on the detail of the encounter with

[1] www.anationalvoice.org
[2] www.youngminds.org.uk

social work we lose some of the background (though see Chapter 11 for more discussion of this). Since we take as our starting point the individual encounter it is not surprising that the frame for the discussion of good practice begins at this interpersonal level. However, social work is not just an interpersonal process. It requires a critical knowledge of political, social, legal, professional and organisational contexts and these might not be apparent in the interpersonal encounter of social worker and service user. Like the one-ninth of the iceberg that is visible, are there eight-ninths of good practice that the explorations in this book fail to bring to light? We cannot know, but hope that the reader will agree that even this supposedly exposed part of practice is in urgent need of more visibility.

We hope that the sharp relief of the stories is not too remote from context, but we aim to counter-balance those texts that are overwhelmingly concerned with abstracted contexts and are blurred around the detail. Returning to the notion of choreography referred to in the Preface, 'how we represent ourselves and others is something to be worked at' (Taylor, 2006: 194) and we can only speculate what other influences were critical to the stories and to the telling of the events. As the authors who assisted in the construction of these stories, we feel confident that the people who gave their time and interest did so out of a strong desire to talk about their experiences honestly and directly, and to contribute to improving practices.

Using the book

Everybody has experienced teachers and most people have encountered doctors, but social work is not a universal service and many people's first contact with social work is exactly that. As we noted in the Preface, there are few fictional examples of social work in action, whether literary or televisual, and there are indications that service users have unclear ideas about what social workers do, so that they learn most of this during the actual process of working with a social worker (Kadushin, 1996). We hope that the book can paint a picture of social work for the wider population.

These encounters can help readers to consider issues of good practice, whether you dip into one or more stories from time to time, or read through from start to finish. The commentaries which follow on from the stories might serve as additional teaching and learning, or the stories might just speak for themselves. Depending on who you are, you might put yourself into the story and reflect on how you might have experienced the encounter or what you might have done. You might choose to consider a story from a particular perspective, for example, emancipatory practice (Wilkes, 2004). The stories could be used side by side with case vignettes, either from the the current experience of the reader or from the literature (such as Haulotte and Kretzschmaur, 2001).

As authors, we too had an opportunity for reflection in the commentaries which follow each story. These are our attempts to deconstruct the experience from a rather abstract point of view – the process of *social working*. The stories were not recounted with any moral in mind, and yet it is difficult not to convert them readily into morality tales. Reading each story, what can we abstract from it in terms of the processes of social work that are experienced as positive? Whilst specific to the particular story, what is also open to generalisation, tentative though this may be? (See Chapter 11 for more about these generalisations.) Of course, these deconstructions are ours, as the book's authors; subjective, yet emerging from honest listening, which was part of the ethical basis for the book. As the reader, you might prefer to make your own reflections first.

The commentaries are not prescriptions for good practice, not bullet-pointed 'to do' lists, rather an opportunity to present themes and issues for debate. There are sufficient texts telling social workers what they ought to do. We hope it will be refreshing to have a dialogue with these actual encounters and to ponder how and why they were experienced as positive.

2 Learning from Humerah

'When people see me they think "physical disability", but actually it's my mental health'

Humerah uses a wheelchair. However, her main contact is with the mental health services. Her first psychiatric admission was 19 years ago and her first social worker contact a year later when she was sectioned for the first time. Over the past 18 years she has been 'a revolving door', coming in and out of the system periodically. She has been with her current mental health team for eight years. This is multi-professional and includes a psychiatrist and a care coordinator. She has had a variety of social workers and community psychiatric nurses ('I've lost count how many') and, until she was allocated her current social worker, most of the experience had been very negative.

'The mental health services find it difficult to have someone who has insight and is articulate and yet on another level is a complete mess,' says Humerah. 'It doesn't make any sense to them.' It doesn't make sense because when the professionals think 'mental distress' they see people climbing walls, not getting dressed, not able to pay bills. Humerah does not conform to this stereotype. She presents as someone who on one level manages very well, and is described as 'high functioning', yet privately struggles with hearing voices, self-harm and ideas of suicide.

Humerah works in a responsible job. She has lost jobs a couple of times on account of her mental health problems. On one occasion she was admitted to an acute psychiatric ward just a week after an appointment to a new senior position. She spent the first three months going to work from the ward but no one at work knew. She works in the social care field and muses that it is interesting how we don't look down on doctors and nurses when they get ill, yet in social care it seems hard to accept as colleagues people who use services, particularly in senior positions. Workers have clear images of people who use services and though we welcome user involvement, it is a different story if service users also have an identity as professionals and peers. Humerah's team had enormous difficulties in accepting and coping with her mental health problems. Her treatment by her agency at the time was so fraught that she started proceedings for judicial review of her case.

Humerah notes that she became extremely litigious, making frequent written complaints and taking legal action in response to her anger and frustration at the poor service she was receiving. Then two years ago her social worker changed. 'My social work relationship has changed beyond belief,' she muses, then smiles. 'I'm no longer making complaint letters or taking legal action.'

What is the difference? What does her current social worker do which has had such a dramatic impact and which has changed the pattern of 18 years?

Humerah describes the difference as 'I feel she is working with me and wants to find solutions that will work for me'. When asked what this means in practice, she says that her social worker knows when to take the lead and when to back off.

'When I'm having a real wobble I stop my medication. I'm quite a danger to myself, and though I can still somehow go into work the rest of my life is a complete mess and I can't take action to deal with it. Logic goes out of the window.' At these times Humerah's worker will do basic plans which include what to do to stay safe, like giving Humerah a timetable. Humerah knows that, as she appears so competent, it is difficult to understand that there are times when she needs this kind of basic care and control. Her worker will say, 'Humerah, is it time to go into hospital?' or she will say, 'We're going to do this or that, I'm not asking you, I'm telling you.'

Humerah observes that it sounds a real contradiction in terms, that having her worker take this degree of control is, at these times, the right thing for her to do, even an empowering thing. 'They just need to take control – and that's not to give up control forever.' She explains that, though she hates to say it, one of the things that works very well for her is when control is temporarily taken away from her. She regards detention under the Mental Health Act as a necessary evil, indeed, she has been detained over a dozen times. 'It takes control away from me, sets clear boundaries.' Humerah recognises that it is not necessarily going to work for everyone, but it works for her. 'It's saved my life several times.' She knows that logically you would not stop taking medication when you knew what the consequences were, but stopping her medication is the first thing that she does when she is approaching a wobble.

Her social worker knows her triggers, the vulnerable points which are likely to precipitate an episode. Moreover, she does not try to reform her or divert her, but just accepts without making a value judgement. Sometimes the worker acknowledges that 'we've reached a point where we're both stuck'.

I wonder whether Humerah knew early on that things were going to be different with this social worker. She is not certain about this (it is two years since they have been working together), but does remember that the relationship developed very quickly. However, she does remember one aspect of the first session very well. She did say to her social worker that she knew that she was seen as 'a very difficult client', and that before the two of them started running into problems they needed to think about how they could change it. Humerah muses that perhaps this overture should have come from the social worker, to say something like 'I know it hasn't been easy, but ...'. Even so, Humerah appreciated that the social worker did say that she did not mind Humerah getting angry. 'She said she didn't mind me getting angry at her, but she did want me to speak to her first before I went off writing to her manager. That was really good ... It came over to me as, if you've got a complaint and you're not happy with me you need to tell me, and we need to talk about it.' Humerah knew that she could still complain if she wanted to, but that she should first let the worker know if she was not happy with things. This was only fair to the worker.

It seems that communication had completely broken down in Humerah's relationships with previous social workers. She would regularly write letters to the team manager and the head of adult mental health services because she saw no point in talking to the social worker. 'They couldn't see what my issues were and why I might be having difficulties.'

Humerah has severe and enduring mental health problems. She thinks professionals have a real problem because she is not seen as 'deserving'. Ironically, as an articulate person in regular employment she feels that she is seen as not needy enough or deserving. 'I fell outside the needy person category because I don't fit the stereotype of a service user, especially as I work.'

Humerah volunteers that her social worker has told her that she thinks that her journey is going to get worse before it gets better and that it is going to take time. Messengers with this kind of news are not usually popular. No one likes thinking things will get harder, but Humerah says that this social worker helped her understand that unless certain issues were tackled through a mix of therapy and medication, she would not be able to move forward. This came after Humerah had wondered in some distress how come life was actually getting harder, after all these years of mental health services. 'Surely I should be getting better at dealing with it?' The breakthrough for Humerah came when her social worker offered her a metaphor which transformed the way she saw her situation. The social worker said she thought that all Humerah's childhood and adult life she pushed things to the back of the cupboard, just getting on and giving the impression of coping. The cupboard got so crammed she could no longer keep the cupboard doors shut and it all started spilling out. 'When she said that it just clicked.'

I ask Humerah when this happened, how far into the work with the social worker. She cannot remember for sure but surmises that it was probably about three months after the change to this new worker, around Christmas-time, which is a bad time for her.

The social worker is now a team manager, but she has carried on working with Humerah. When I ask Humerah if she and the worker ever disagree about things she puts me in no doubt that they do. For example, there is a really big bone of contention about contact by email. Humerah works in a large open-plan office where privacy is hard to find, so she does not see the phone as an option. 'My worker absolutely refuses to let me have her work email address, and she says that if she lets me have it then she has to let other service users have it.' Humerah says that she knows that they don't have many people in work so there would not be much call on the email and that perhaps it would be useful for others, too. Humerah paced herself and decided to bring the subject up again a couple of months later and when the response was still negative 'we had a humdinger'. She thinks that the funny thing is that it works both ways and her worker sometimes finds it hard to contact her, whereas an email would reach her easily! Also, recently, the worker gave Humerah her mobile number 'but I have never used it'. She acknowledges that she and her worker have different views about which is the more private boundary. They agree to disagree.

Another point of disagreement arose around Humerah's CPA (she explains that this stands for Care Programme Approach). She had disclosed something private to her worker, not expecting that she would make it 'public'. Humerah understands that some information needs to be shared with other workers, but if the worker had explained that she was going to mention this information, Humerah would have had the choice as to whether the friend who accompanied her at CPA meetings should be privy to it or leave the room, since the friend was not aware of this information. 'Afterwards I was really angry with her. My worker said although this isn't a family relationship, it is like family relationship, and you get angry and you fall out, but that's OK, that's fine. I could have kicked her for saying that, but actually I thought, yes that's probably right.'

The question of balance is very important, especially around this issue of control. For example, Humerah could remember a while ago she said to her social worker that she thought her care budget should be cut because she wasn't using support workers as much as she used to. What happened was that the social worker said OK, but actually she didn't report back to the head of adult mental health services and she kept Humerah's budget at exactly the same cost 'because she knew that it wouldn't be too long before it would need to be upped again'. It was a lot harder to increase a budget than to keep it steady, and she had known that Humerah would need the increased budget at some point. Humerah appreciated that it was the worker's job to know what was and was not possible with her agency and did not mind that she had taken the decision into her own hands. 'It comes down to her taking the lead when I need her to.' The important thing, too, is that they can talk about it afterwards.

Humerah has talked about the times it has been important for the worker to take control, but what about the other side of the balance. Did she have an example of the worker letting go? Humerah says that recently she was offered supported housing and she had a lot of discussion with her worker about the pros and cons. She had eventually decided not to move and this was entirely her own decision, with her social worker not offering an opinion but just helping her to come to her own decision.

Another example is Humerah's decision not to have any 'advance directives'. Humerah explains that these are written instructions which people can make when they are feeling well to cover what they would like to happen 'when I go into a wobble'. These would certainly make life easier, but Humerah has made it clear that she would not care what she had agreed when she is well; if she was on a wobble it would become meaningless. 'The social worker has accepted that advance directives are not for me, she's said "fine".'

Humerah's social worker is Asian. Before any assumptions can be drawn she declares emphatically that she does not believe in 'matching', that is, putting social workers and service users together on the basis of race. Humerah declares that what is so good about her present social worker is 'the combination of skills and expertise she brings *combined with* her knowledge as an Asian woman'. Humerah says that the fact that her worker is an Asian female is not the most important factor, but a good Asian worker can make it easier; she can think of circumstances when this might be disadvantageous (for example, if there was an assumption that they were 'the same', or they held fixed views about culture). In fact, they are from very different communities with dissimilar backgrounds in every other respect than the fact that they are both Asian. So, the ethnicity is not the deciding factor, but in this case it has turned out to make a difference.

Humerah has no family involved and there is a 'full stop' as soon as they are mentioned. The social worker 'has accepted my family situation – it isn't an extended family – and she hasn't insisted on involvement'. It is another example of her respecting Humerah's wishes and letting her have control. 'Some social workers are pushing all the time to get your family involved, even when it's clear you don't want it or it's not appropriate.'

There is no timescale to the worker's involvement with Humerah because of the nature of her recurring mental health problems. She sees Humerah about once a fortnight – more when necessary. She coordinates Humerah's care plan and also meets with her therapist from time to time. Humerah explains that her worker used to be a part-time counsellor at a GP surgery and, although she is not doing 'counselling' with Humerah, she thinks the counselling skills which the worker brings are a help. 'When I'm very distressed she doesn't push it, just gives me space.'

Humerah has physical care needs, too. Her social worker integrates the physical and mental health care. Humerah talks about how they tried to close her mental health case some while back (before her current worker) and place her with the physical disability team. 'They said, "that's your primary diagnosis, physical disability, and that's the team you have to go to". My argument was very clear that my physical condition doesn't require a lot of care, but it's my mental health condition that makes the roof fall in over and over again.' Humerah had to appeal and meet with the head of services. Her previous social worker had always said that this or that could not be paid for out of the physical disability budget. Humerah became very involved with the detail of budgets and trying to strategise and work round the system, as administered by her social workers.

When she appealed and met with the Head of Services, she asked again about what budget this help and that help would come from. 'They said, "it shouldn't matter to you about the budget" and, you know, that was absolutely right. What's important is getting the care, not who pays for it. That's what *they* are paid to worry about!'

'My social worker recognises the importance of work for me, and her support for me to be able to work is a major plus. She thinks outside the usual boxes when working with mental health service users. By offering support and flexibility that fits around my employment it enables me to retain my identity and sense of self-worth.'

What we can learn from Humerah's story

Humerah's story throws light on many different aspects of good practice. Before you read our commentary below, perhaps you would like to make a list of your own headlines. What are the important messages from your reading of Humerah's positive experience of social work?

Below we present 12 themes from Humerah's story. See how they compare with your own list.

1 Recognising, and resisting, the weight of history

Humerah became extremely litigious, making frequent written complaints and taking legal action.

Our initial encounter with a person who is, or may become, a service user may not be their first experience of our service. Even when it is the first contact, there will always be some prior beliefs and impressions, accurate or not, of what social work is and what social workers do.

People are likely to respond to us as the embodiment of the experience of the service so far (or their stereotypes about social work), not for who we are. We have some indefinable responsibility for what went before, so trying to deny it or slough it off is also not acceptable. We accept that there has been a bad service (if there has) and, without sackcloth and ashes, accept our part in the wider system of social work services. People may not like the kind of person they have become ('I became extremely litigious'), just as parents can find themselves surprised and dismayed when they hear themselves say things that they had never imagined themselves capable of ('wait til your father gets home'; 'I wish you'd never been born'), service users are not necessarily happy with what they feel they have become as a result of their experiences.

2 Breaking through stereotypes

'When people see me they think "physical disability", but actually it's my mental health.'

Humerah confounds many stereotypes. The obvious physical first impression (a disabled person) leads to a categorisation that is not based on Humerah's own priorities. Beyond that, once she enabled the professionals to see her mental health priorities, she does not conform to any of the 'types' that professionals use to order the world of mental disorder. Of all the domains of social work practice mental health is the one most likely to be dominated by medical models of understanding; these rely on diagnostic tools by which professionals can place their own sense of order on what is so often a chaotic world. Social working means moving beyond these categories and not relying on them to give much more than a shorthand account of a cluster of behaviours and attributes. This is one good reason why social workers are social workers first and mental health professionals second – they should retain their scepticism of labels and not come to rely on them.

Ironically, as an articulate person with insight, Humerah also challenged the mental health system's definition of someone who is deserving. Social working disavows moral accountancy and helps us to see Humerah as a person with a unique set of experiences, behaviours, needs and wants. If there is to be a rationing of services it is not to be achieved by attributing less moral weight to some people than to others, based on a judgement about how well they fit a stereotype.

Humerah experienced her social worker as someone who broke through the stereotypes.

Humerah crosses yet another significant boundary – the one between professional and service user. In one part of her life she is a well-respected member of the social care profession, in another she is a high-profile service user, and she crosses those boundaries back and forth regularly. As she notes, we do not feel that a doctor who falls ill has somehow failed or is contravening a social code, and yet this has been her experience of not living up to the ideal of the coping professional. Like other social groups who cross boundaries where hard lines have been drawn (for example, dual heritage people, bisexuals) people who are service users and professionals break the taboo and hegemony of Cartesian dualism (everything must be either P or not P). Humerah experiences her social worker as someone who does not make these dualist judgements.

3 Responding to different rhythms

'My social worker knows when to take the lead and when to back off.'

Humerah knows that she has different needs at different times. There are times when she is lucid and managing her life well, other times when she is a great danger to herself and, of course, times when she is moving between these two states. The social worker must respond to the different rhythms in Humerah's life, taking her lead from Humerah, even when this means taking the lead for her. Managing this paradox – of taking the lead from the service user and sometimes *for* the service user, is intricate. We need a repertoire of responsive and systematic communications to work with these different rhythms (Reid and Epstein, 1973). Good practice is based on the ability to use both these kinds of communication and to weave them together in unique combinations with every encounter.

Humerah's rhythms have a pattern. The social worker recognises the evidence, such as Humerah stopping her medication, that a different rhythm may be about to emerge. In her relationship with her social worker, Humerah notes the change by pointing to the evidence: 'I'm no longer making complaint letters or taking legal action.' Both Humerah and her worker search the evidence that might indicate changes, patterns, rhythms in the work.

4 Sharing control

'They just need to take control – and that's not to give up control forever.'

When we read Humerah's account we become aware of the importance of control. Understandably, students new to social work can incline to interpret empowerment as 'giving control to the service user'; however, Humerah's story demonstrates how complex the question of control is. There are several episodes in which Humerah makes a central reference to the notion of control: being given a timetable when she is approaching 'a wobble'; making a decision over whether to move; making changes in her care budget; whether to have advance directives; release of confidential information at a meeting; which 'label' (physical disability/mental health) to prioritise and, therefore, which team to be allocated to; which budgets the care should come from; whether email contact is permissible.

What is striking is the wide range of results. If we were to imagine a continuum from one end (zero) in which Humerah has no control to the other (ten) in which she has total control, we can see that these episodes cover the whole range. We might naively assume that Humerah would only be happy with those episodes which were scoring eight, nine and ten. Yet she is positive about the whole continuum; even the episode which brings her into most disagreement with her worker, the email decision in which the worker decides to keep total control, does not strike a major blow to the relationship and results in an agreement to disagree. How does this happen?

Let us think of the continuum not as static but, rather like a swingometer, there is a large arrow which is capable of being moved up to the one side and back up to the other. Whose hand is on the arrow? In other words, how are the decisions about the degree of control made? A naive response would be 'of course, empowerment means that it is the service user's hand moving the arrow'. This would be wrong again. The fact is that both the service user and the social worker must share this responsibility; because of their relative power and professional expertise, the social worker has an added responsibility to explore this process, so that the notion of control and how it can be used is central to the encounter.

5 Agreeing groundrules

'The social worker said she didn't mind me getting angry at her, but she did want me to speak to her first before I went off writing to her manager.'

The control issues raised in the preceding section point to the significance of groundrules early in the encounter. The theory and practice of groundrules is relatively well developed in family work and groupwork (Doel, 2006), less so in individual work. Groundrules provide a framework for the working relationship (the outcome) and an experience of the working style of the social worker (the process). The groundrules should be used as a compass to guide the work and a relatively objective reference point to use when the journey is difficult and stressful. Groundrules help the people in any encounter to set out their stalls, to barter and trade, to anticipate potential problems and agree acceptable responses to them. They should be revisited from time to time to check their purpose and relevance; if they are not working as they should, the bearings should be re-set. In some working methods, such as task-centred practice, the groundrules are formalised into a written agreement (Marsh and Doel, 2005).

It is Humerah who first broaches groundrules by noting that she knows she is seen as a difficult client. This opens the way to a discussion about their expectations of one another and Humerah's assertiveness is matched by her social worker's (for a wider discussion of assertiveness in social work see McBride, 1998). Probably, the worker should have formalised this rather more, but her openness and directness impress Humerah sufficiently for her to feel that things will be different with this worker.

6 Using personal attributes skilfully

The social worker helped her understand that unless certain issues were tackled through a mix of therapy and medication, she would not be able to move forward.

It is a matter of contention as to whether personal attributes can be acquired, but interpersonal skills can certainly be learned – such as communicated empathy (Nerdrum and Lundquist, 1995). Social workers have their own styles, coloured by their personal attributes. Whether we successfully communicate these attributes depends on skill and regular feedback; for example, we may *feel* accepting, but is what we say and do *experienced* as acceptance? Above all, we need to be genuinely curious about these things.

From Humerah's account of her social worker, there are many attributes which she appears to have appreciated. We will highlight three of these.

Acceptance   Humerah's social worker is not trying to reform her. The desire to change the world may be one of the social work motivations but, without wishing to curb enthusiasm and ambition, reforming zeal is actually seldom attractive (witness successive UK governments). Accepting a person for who they are might be a very new and liberating experience in itself. Unconditional acceptance does not mean approval of everything the person *does*, but it signals an understanding of the person as a whole. Humerah's worker is realistic about what is possible and not possible for her; she holds out hope but not an idealised future.

Fairness   The social worker quietly ignores Humerah's suggestion that she might change her care budget; she rather more noisily refuses to communicate by email; she mistakenly mentions a matter of confidence in front of Humerah's friend. These are all episodes which could have resulted in major fractures in the working relationship. The fact that they did not is perhaps a result of the sense of fairness that she has managed to create. Humerah feels confident that her worker has her best interests at heart and that at all times is balanced and even-handed in her dealings. She is denying Humerah communication by email, but she denies *all other service users* this facility, too, so Humerah knows that – right or wrong – she is not singled out for different treatment and she knows that the worker's decision is based on reasoning, even if it is different from her own reasoning.

Directness   Directness in itself could be brutal and bullying. It is the combination of attributes and the context in which they are given expression which leads to the positive experience of social work. The worker's directness is expressed in the context of her *concern* for Humerah. This same sense of concern could lead another worker towards shielding and protectiveness (and, indeed, in other contexts perhaps this social worker would have sensed the need to curb her attribute of directness). In the context of the precariousness of Humerah's situation, taken with the strength of the working relationship, the worker took the risk of directness.

So, these attributes help to build qualities we might look for in a good working relationship – trust, confidence and reliability.

7 Taking risks and provoking a re-think

'When she said that, it just clicked.'

Risk assessment has become big, some might say dominating, in social work practice. Alongside the high profile risks of life and limb (which are present in the work with Humerah), are the smaller acts of risk-taking associated with the working relationship. In addition to the safety nets in place for Humerah when she wobbled, this worker took the risk of challenging her to see her situation in a way that no previous worker had achieved.

Offering interpretations and insights carries many risks. They can fall wide of the mark, thus emphasising the worker's distance rather than their 'being alongside'. The insight might be accurate but unacceptable or mistimed, opening a door that is shut for good reason. Humerah does not state it explicitly, but we can infer that the *way* in which the insight is offered is important, certainly if it is not to be felt as a presumption. Offering a metaphor softens the risk because it leaves room for the listener to make their own reconstruction: 'she thought that all Humerah's childhood and adult life she pushed things to the back of the cupboard, just getting on and giving the impression of coping. The cupboard got so crammed she could no longer keep the cupboard doors shut and it all started spilling out'. The worker is not telling Humerah something that she did not already know at some level, but the metaphor of the cupboard unleashed Humerah's understanding, helped her to see the situation in a new light. It is interesting to note that the worker does not need to know the detail of what is in the cupboard to construct this image.

The worker's knowledge of Humerah went beyond a critical appraisal of her situation to an understanding of how best to communicate this knowledge. Cupboards and wardrobes have a strong place in our mythology, especially childhood mythologies, and this probably makes it all the more powerful as an image for Humerah to re-think her situation. Some people find metaphor easier to construct and deconstruct than others. Humerah's imagination and intelligence is a strength which helped her respond to metaphor.

8 Acknowledging mistakes

Humerah had disclosed something private to her worker, not expecting that she would make it 'public'.

If there was ever any doubt in the reader's mind about the complexity of social working this should have disappeared by now. It is small wonder that there are mistakes, even when the worker is as skilled and respected by the service user as Humerah's. Handling information is difficult and, as we see from other people's stories in this book, it is often felt to be a crucial element of positive practice. Sometimes social workers have to make an explicit choice to reveal information; at others, as in this instance, a moment's thoughtlessness means that others become privy to knowledge that was given in confidence. Humerah's friend had been absorbed into the meeting and the information was shared with thoughtlessness about this person's presence.

Whilst avoiding a *mea culpa,* there is a strong case for an apology to be made when a mistake of this kind occurs. A defensive worker might try to shift blame – 'it wouldn't have happened if you hadn't insisted bringing your friend along'. Interestingly, Humerah's worker neither apologises nor blames but likens the situation to a family where people get angry, fall out, and that is fine. Humerah is annoyed at this response ('I could have kicked her for saying that'); and yet she continues with the thought that 'actually, yes, that's probably right'.

9 Considering difference and similarity

'The fact that my worker is an Asian female [like me] is not the most important factor, but a good Asian worker can make it easier.'

It would be easy to assume that Humerah's positive response is largely due to the fact that she and the social worker are both Asian women. 'Matching' social worker and service user is a hot issue, and Humerah's story seems to support the benefits of matching. However, this is based on assumptions that need unpacking. The first is that Humerah and her worker are so similar. As Asian women living and working in England they will have experiences in common, but in fact they are from very different communities with dissimilar backgrounds in every other respect than the fact that they are both Asian.

The second assumption is that Humerah identifies the 'match' as critical, which she does not. She describes the combination of factors as *contributing* to her positive experience. It is a topic which needs more evidence, but Devore and Schlesinger (1991: 191) demonstrated that there can be disadvantages to a worker and service user duo from similar backgrounds. They illustrate this with the example of a Jewish social worker whose stereotypes of her own people led her to be oppressively judgemental about Jewish service users.

We do not know from Humerah's story to what extent she and the social worker discussed their similarities and their differences. What we can be certain about is that these should be openly referred to ... 'I recognise that I am seeing this situation as a man ...' etc. Differences, where they exist, may be celebrated as having the potential to bring other perspectives rather than necessarily creating distance ... the metaphor of unlike magnetic poles attracting.

Achieving a mix of similarity and difference in the people working with a service user may be important. One study found that young people particularly valued mentors who shared and were willing to discuss similar backgrounds and experiences (Philip et al., 2004). They felt these relationships differed from those they had with other professionals and adults, where it might be appropriate for the young people to experience differences and role distance.

10 Keeping personal ideologies in check

'Some social workers are pushing all the time to get your family involved, even when it's clear you don't want it or it's not appropriate.'

'Family' does not register on Humerah's radar and she was pleased that her social worker accepted this. Whatever the particular bugbear, a social worker's profound belief in the value of *x*, *y* or *z* can sometimes drive their practice in the opposite direction to the service user. This is a difficult issue, because social workers need their own 'professional compasses' to help them keep their bearings and give professional purpose to their encounters. They hold beliefs and these are sometimes fundamental to their practice; they have knowledge which they should use to inform their practice. However, the belief and the knowledge should be held tentatively, always open to new and different evidence that might challenge existing beliefs and modify current knowledge.

11 Managing the agency

It was the worker's job to know what was and was not possible with her agency.

There is much made of case management, but for some service users it is *the agency* that their social worker needs most to manage. Certainly, one of the authors' first experience of qualified practice was in a highly dysfunctional agency in which the workers' main task was to protect the clients from the agency. When Humerah was dissatisfied with her experience of social work she tried to manage her relationship with the agency directly, and we can imagine the kind of reputation she acquired with the agency. Perhaps agencies with 'difficult' clients need to think about this. Since her experience of social work has turned so positive Humerah sees the management of the agency as the worker's responsibility, as indeed it is. This suggests that service users do not necessarily require details of, for example, the composition of teams (Meddings and Perkins, 1999).

The social worker's practice does not occur in a vacuum, though the stories in this book do suggest that the individual social worker is very important and can transcend their agency. We do not know whether the social workers in these stories found their agencies supportive or not, but we do know that in Humerah's case the agency stayed the same and the only change was the worker. Agencies might care to note that Humerah makes mention of her social worker's experience as a counsellor as positive (her thoughts about her social worker's training in case management go unnoted). She is keen to emphasise, too, that she never felt 'counselled' and did not want to be, but that the worker was able to draw on some of these skills.

12 Believing it is possible to make a difference

'Then two years ago my social worker changed [and] my social work relationship has changed beyond belief.'

We leave the most powerful and positive message to emerge from Humerah's story to the last: the fact that it is possible for one social worker to make a difference, and an enormous one at that. Without wishing to put too much responsibility on the shoulders of one person, we learn from Humerah that even the weight of 18 years' negative experience can be transformed speedily by just one person. That must give all of us pause for thought – service users, students, practitioners (novice and experienced), managers and educators.

The rest of the themes in this commentary have provided pointers to the 'how' this social worker achieved such a turnaround. Here we merely pause to recognise the very fact. We should pause, too, and remind ourselves that the consequence is not that Humerah 'gets better'; indeed, her social worker is blunt with her that things are likely to get worse first. Humerah's mental health needs and difficulties do not disappear as a consequence of this new experience of positive social working. What happens is that Humerah no longer has the mental health system as one of her problems. She has someone she can now trust to mediate with that system on her behalf, and whom she feels is sufficiently powerful and empowered to do this; someone who has given her faith that she and her interests will be looked after her when she is not able to do this. How George III could have benefited from Humerah's social worker during his bouts of madness!

Summary of learning points from Humerah's story

1 Recognising, and resisting, the weight of history
2 Breaking through stereotypes
3 Responding to different rhythms
4 Sharing control
5 Agreeing groundrules
6 Using personal attributes skilfully
7 Taking risks and provoking a re-think
8 Acknowledging mistakes
9 Considering difference and similarity
10 Keeping personal ideologies in check
11 Managing the agency
12 Believing it is possible to make a difference

3 Learning from Mandy

'She gave space for me to talk about my situation from my point of view'

Mandy first had contact with a social worker from social services about nine months ago. Three months before that, after a violent argument, she and her husband had separated, leaving the three children in Mandy's care. It was when one of the children discovered Mandy in a drunken stupor that she and the family realised that they needed help. Social services were briefly involved, then a social worker from a voluntary organisation began to work with the family, specifically around the difficulties arising from the behaviour of the oldest boy, Kevin, aged 12.

The first thing that Mandy appreciated was the speed with which her social worker became involved. 'I needed help there and then, and that's when it came. It was really important to have someone quick.' The worker was able to be involved with Mandy and her family at the significant point of crisis, and this was all-important for Mandy. In contrast, another organisation had said that they could supply a volunteer worker, 'but I'm still waiting'.

The social worker talked with Mandy about what had brought things to this point, and she gave space for Mandy to talk about her situation from her point of view. Mandy realised that she had been putting the lid on things. Her mother died many years ago and she is not close to her father. She feels close to her sister, but the sister has a very busy job, lives at some distance, and couldn't give the level of support that Mandy needed. 'I can't believe now that I went to such extreme lengths – bottling it all up like that.' Talking with the social worker helped Mandy to put things into perspective and to reflect how bad things had become. 'We sat and talked. Just me and the social worker the first time. I talked about Kevin's behaviour, too, and my husband's attitude.'

Mandy was finding Kevin's outbursts a huge strain, especially since Kevin's response to his parents' separation was to use it to hurt them both as much as he could. 'I needed someone to get involved – I was getting nowhere fast.'

The social worker provided practical help by discussing different methods that Mandy could use to manage Kevin's behaviour. They worked with varying success, but at least Mandy felt she was regaining some control of the situation. 'It were really helpful advice, you know, sending Kevin to his room. I have to take time out – go into the kitchen and put the kettle on. Kevin knows how to wind me up.'

Mandy also appreciated that the worker also took Kevin for sessions, too. A student from the agency was also now involved with Kevin and taking him and his younger brother for treats to the local leisure centre, and to provide some respite for Mandy during school holidays.

Mandy talks about the strategies that she has learned through the work with her social worker. 'It were hard and still is ... I'm still learning.'

What was it that the social worker could provide that friends or neighbours couldn't? Mandy recounts how she was getting support from two friends on the estate. 'They were trying to help me by telling Kevin what he should be doing and he didn't like that. They could see that he was getting me down and they tried to help me out.' She sees less of these friends now, partly because of Kevin's resentful reaction to them. 'They would tell him what to do and he wouldn't like that. The social worker focuses more on the *strategies*.'

Mandy also values the regularity of her contact with the worker. At this stage she doesn't know how much longer she will need to see her, but she still feels in the middle of it all and still relies on the worker's *presence*. 'I get the chance to talk to her – I see her every week, and I like that it's regular. I like to know when she's coming. It's like, well, thank God, she's here! ... I think to myself "The social worker is here now so we can deal with it".' Mandy describes how she can hold on to stuff when she knows that she has a time to see her worker in the near future, or she can phone, too.

Talking with the social worker has helped Mandy to develop certain insights into her relationships which would not have come otherwise. For example, she realises that when her husband left she began to treat Kevin, as the oldest boy, as another adult, someone to talk to in the absence of adult company. 'It's at night time when you're on your own that you really miss having a partner – even if you kept the kids up all night it's not the same as having an adult.' Mandy now sees that this is not appropriate, unfair on Kevin, even though he himself often acts as if he is 'the man in the house'. Although there is still a long way to go, Mandy feels that she *knows* more about what the problems are and that her social worker has introduced her to the idea of boundaries and their importance.

'I find my social worker helpful coming because I didn't have anybody to tell things who was an adult.'

What we can learn from Mandy's story

Mandy's story throws light on many different aspects of good practice. Before you read our analysis below, perhaps you would like to make a list of your own headlines. What are the important messages from your reading of Mandy's positive experience of social work?

Below we present seven themes from Mandy's story. See how they compare with your own list.

1 Responding speedily

'It was really important to have someone quick.'

One of the authors remembers an area manager who operated on the belief that most situations, left alone, sort themselves. This *laissez-faire* approach resulted in much more work over time, with the relentless accumulation of stapled re-referral forms. When contact was finally made, workers had to manage the additional problem of the anger at the agency's lack of responsiveness. Of course, there are times when a social worker arrives to find that the situation has blown over, but for each of these occasions there are many in which a prompt response makes all the difference.

Mandy is very specific that the speed of her worker's involvement was critical. For the worker's part, it means that she is able to make use of the crisis and the heightened motivation that it can induce. Working with Mandy whilst she is in the midst of the events means the worker can experience these first hand, even become a part of them and integrate them into the work. Any changes in belief, attitude and behaviour are likely to be most effective if they can be understood in the immediate context of the need for these changes and the crisis provides an opportunity to rehearse these changes (Trevithick, 2005). The need for change is often at its most transparent during a crisis and if the social worker delays responding attitudes are likely to have slipped back or hardened. Finally, responding promptly is an indication that the social worker has the wherewithal to deliver and that he or she bothers.

2 Making time to talk

'She gave space for me to talk about my situation from my point of view.'

The response to crisis should not itself be at crisis pitch. The heightened emotion that accompanies a crisis is best met with calm and reflection. Mandy describes her social worker as giving her 'space'. With the sole responsibility of the care of the children, Mandy has perhaps found it difficult to find time for herself. She is likely to feel judged by everyone around her and perhaps anticipates a lecture, or worse, from the social worker about her being drunk whilst the children were in her care. Instead, she finds that the social worker creates a space for Mandy to tell her story, and she wants to find out how things feel and look from Mandy's point of view.

This might seem little more than common sense but, as emerges when Mandy later describes her friends' intervention, the partisan support that most untrained people offer frequently has only short-term benefit. The urge to judge ('you've been badly treated') or to offer solutions ('you know what you ought to do now ...') are common responses from neighbours and friends and, though they offer one kind of support, the emotion and weight of judgement that accompanies this support can leave the person feeling even more burdened. What the social worker does is to offer a neutral, quiet zone in which Mandy tells her story without the clutter of others' commentaries. Paradoxically, though it is neutral, it can be experienced as a stronger form of support than the banshee of partisans.

3 Giving hands-on practical support

'The social worker focuses more on the strategies.'

Listening to a person's story is the first step. It enables both Mandy and her social worker to understand the situation better and to take stock of it. In fact, Mandy comes to a realisation of how bad things are. In some circumstances this could be the prelude to despair, but she is motivated to move to the next stage and her story suggests that this arises from the confidence she feels in her new worker. The worker, too, is able to take the next steps, move on from creating a space to doing something with it.

The social worker uses her practical knowledge and skills to teach Mandy some quite specific techniques to improve the situation. It is not the intention of the worker to use these techniques on Mandy's behalf, rather for Mandy to learn them and to encourage her to try them. Mandy appreciates the fact that the social worker also worked directly with her son, Kevin, and extended this work to a student in the agency who provides practical respite for Mandy by sharing some of the parenting responsibilities during the summer school break.

Mandy is realistic that the learning is hard work and that it continues. Some of the techniques work better than others and there are setbacks. Even so, she has confidence in the overall process and in the social worker's knowledge, skill and care.

4 Maintaining regular contact

'I like to know when she's coming. It's like, well, thank God, she's here'

Following the prompt response to the first crisis, Mandy likes the way her social worker keeps regular contact. At present this is weekly and by appointment. This means that Mandy can anticipate the social worker's visit and keep a hold on her anxieties in the knowledge that she only has to wait for a certain time. Social workers should not under-estimate the importance of regular contacts at agreed times – they often mean that the time between contacts can be longer because the person is confident that the appointments will not be cancelled or postponed. This kind of regular structure is integral to some methods of practice, such as task-centred practice (Marsh and Doel, 2005). Although it is dif-ficult to isolate particular aspects of a holistic practice, it is reasonable to assume that regular and anticipated access is important to the suc-cess of this method.

People who have experienced unreliable adults during much of their life may take some time before they can trust that the social worker is not going to perpetuate this pattern. If the social worker can set a pattern of reliability and regularity from the start, the service user can accept those occasions when a worker is delayed or has to postpone. The broken pattern will be seen as the aberration and not the norm.

How social workers create the steady working patterns that lead to the confidence of service users is another question. Most social work-ers in the UK do not work as independent clinicians and the climate in their agencies plays a significant part in helping or hindering reliabil-ity. However, there can be striking differences between workers within one agency or even one team, so we can also infer that contrasting working styles, time management techniques and degrees of assertive-ness lead to different levels of reliability. Although these are very basic factors, we are short of good research evidence to explain the differ-ences and their impact.

5 Gaining insights

Mandy feels that she knows more about the problems.

As well as gaining a greater grasp on *what* to do, Mandy is also achiev-ing a better understanding of *why* her situation is as it is. The social worker could have merely taught Mandy a set of behaviour manage-ment techniques, which Mandy could have faithfully reproduced. However, positive social working goes beyond a mechanistic approach. At its best it can encourage insight, a new understanding of one's situ-ation, seeing it from a different perspective. We use the word 'encour-age' because this notion of insight is a powerful one and it can be misused. Social workers determined that their clients should experience 'insight', whatever, can then explain the client's anger and rejection of the so-called insight as defensiveness. Mandy gives no suggestion that she either experienced or would value this kind of interpretative intervention. We can infer from Mandy's experience that the insight should arise from the person themselves, almost as a by-product of the social working, rather than donated by a magician-social worker. Insights offered by one person to another can be wide of the mark or poorly timed (though, as we saw in Humerah's story, they can occasionally work, especially when delivered through a metaphor).

Mandy's insight centres on her relationships, especially with Kevin, the son whose behaviour is increasingly aggressive and angry. The journey she has taken with her social worker has helped Mandy to see how she had looked to her 12-year-old son as a substitute partner. Her need for adult company after her husband left the house, and the tendency of an eldest son to slip into the 'man of the house' role, led her to place an unrealistic load on her son, just at the time when he was feeling hurt by his parents' behaviour and resentful about their decision to part. We can see how the 'cheer crowd' of supporters (i.e. Mandy's friends) are unlikely to induce this kind of reflective insight, though this is not to deny them a valuable supporting role of a kind that social workers cannot fulfil.

Our own insight into social working from Mandy's story is that it is false to try to see reason and emotion as somehow separate and oppositional, external performance and internal motivation somehow not connected (see Howe and Hinings, 1995, for an exploration of reason and emotion in social work). Mandy's experience highlights how social work must connect the two.

6 Avoiding blame

Mandy now sees that this is not appropriate and unfair on Kevin to treat him as an adult.

Mandy's insight is entirely non-blaming. In this she takes her lead from the social worker. It is entirely understandable that she turned to Kevin in this way; entirely understandable, but wrong. Because she developed the insight herself, it emerged at the right time for her, and in a way that she could accept. Her social worker models a non-blaming approach in the neutral zone described earlier. Although Mandy's cheer crowd are cheering for her, they are nevertheless reinforcing the world of blame. They are vociferous about the blame lying with her husband, but in so forcefully allocating blame the belief that there is blame to be allocated is reinforced; in quieter moments, when the cheer crowd have left, perhaps Mandy reflects on whether some of that blame does in fact attach itself to her.

The social worker has introduced a different paradigm which does not dole out blame. Certainly, consequences are considered and the work is bounded by a moral framework (for example, that it is not right to expect Kevin to be a substitute adult), but the discourse is not focused on weighing the respective responsibilities for the problems. In addition to the reliability, resourcefulness and care that we have already noted, this new paradigm by which actions are evaluated and planned is likely to be new to the service user. We do not know from Mandy's story to what extent the social worker has been explicit about these more philosophical issues, but practice methods should include active reflection on these processes.

7 Modelling a supportive adult, not a substitute partner

The social worker introduced her to the idea of boundaries and their importance.

The social worker is a reliable, resourceful and caring adult. Encountering this kind of person at this time of crisis in her life has been more valuable to Mandy than even the social worker might imagine. The only person who could perhaps have provided this kind of support is her sister, but she is very busy and lives at a distance. The social worker has a difficult balance to achieve. She wants to provide Mandy with the experience of a dependable adult, but not one upon whom she becomes dependent. It is true that, early in the crisis, the social worker should expect Mandy to feel some dependency. It is a vulnerable time and the social worker must seem like a life-raft in a terrible storm. However, from the beginning of their relationship, Mandy knows that this is a temporary measure and that the social worker's role is, like the raft, to help convey Mandy to a different place in her life, a place where she will no longer need it. The social worker provides Mandy with a reliable adult who cares about her situation, but all their work is geared towards helping to build Mandy's own capability, first to handle her own feelings, then to face her son's behaviour, and later to begin to rebuild her adult relationships. It is a transfer of the worker's resourcefulness to Mandy.

Positive social work requires the ability to become close to someone without losing sight of the overall goals. Some practitioners find this kind of closeness uncomfortable, yet the testimony of the service users in this book suggests that the people who provide a positive experience of social work are those who go the extra mile, are capable of this closeness whilst always working towards their own departure.

Summary of learning points from Mandy's story

1 Responding speedily
2 Making time to talk
3 Giving hands-on practical support
4 Maintaining regular contact
5 Gaining insights
6 Avoiding blame
7 Modelling a supportive adult, not a substitute partner

4 Learning from Mrs Corbett

'At one point she took over marvellously, but it's OK because I feel in charge'

Mrs Corbett was a teacher before she retired. She had a long and happy marriage to her husband, Harold. She had recently been to a public meeting of a Carers' Group and had been surprised at the haranguing the social workers received. Although it was not easy to go against the flow, she stood up and said how very grateful she was to the social workers and that hers had been a positive experience.

Indeed, her first experience of a social worker was about five years ago. Mrs Corbett had tripped on the bus and had gone to hospital, but the cut on her leg would not heal. She had to return to hospital, and whilst she was there, Harold had a stroke and he was admitted to the same hospital. 'We became known as "The Corbetts!"' she laughed. Mrs Corbett's first social worker, 'tore through the paperwork and insisted on help coming to the house, and arranging meals over the weekend.' However, the experience of coming home to 'help' was an added trauma. 'Harold and I were a very private pair, and we knew we just had to overcome it and give our keys over. But when we came back from the hospital there were two people, two strangers, sitting in our front room. They wanted to do their best, but we were in a state of shock.'

Mr and Mrs Corbett had home care for several months and Mrs Corbett still has someone coming in who helps her to take a bath safely. 'It's OK because I feel in charge. When we came back from hospital and there were those two people sitting in our home I was feeling terribly vulnerable.'

What she particularly likes about her current (second) social worker is how she listens with great care. For example, Mrs Corbett was unhappy about the care a particular agency supplied for Harold, and the social worker listened to her concerns and acted on them. 'She managed to change the care. She could see that Harold was agitated. She was calm about the situation. She dealt with it.' Mrs Corbett does not underestimate the difficulty that the social worker had in making this seemingly simple change. 'She had something of a battle. But the new person who came made good porridge and I never could! And Harold loved his porridge.'

Mrs Corbett knew that both her social workers had experienced unhappiness. She felt that, in their case, this had helped them to become people who give, rather than making them bitter or disappointed. For Mrs Corbett, it helped that they had divulged something of themselves and it made them more human. This humanity was also evident in the way that 'my first social worker would say "Oh, this is a load of rubbish!" when something just wasn't right'. Not pretending that the system is perfect, but also judging what is possible and what is not, is an important skill for social workers.

Mrs Corbett's main concern has always been one of her need for independence and to be in charge, yet also to experience support in this. She recognises the need for workers to have this balance of independence and support, too. In passing, she mentions a friend who has a daughter who has become a social worker but didn't want to work for a certain local authority 'because she didn't want to be thrown to the wolves'. Social workers, too, have a need for a certain amount of independence and proper support to use it competently.

It is important for the social worker to see the person as a whole person and not just as 'a service user'. This means listening and talking more widely than the central reason for the contact. 'The social workers knew Harold was an intelligent man, through our conversations.' Mrs Corbett proudly shows a photograph of her husband in his earlier years, a handsome man in control of his life. 'They could anticipate if Harry was getting over-anxious dealing with these various people coming in.'

It is interesting that, though Mrs Corbett starts from a fiery position of independence, she moves on to an understanding, even a welcoming, of control sometimes being exercised for her. 'What impressed me was the lovely way that my social worker could take over at times of great stress, and in a very nice way. At one point she took over marvellously – she would just deal with it. At times I felt I was going quite mad. She could anticipate.' With the growth of trust, Mrs Corbett could welcome her social worker making some of the decisions for her some of the time. There was always the trust that they would be the right decisions and that control would come back to her as soon as she had the energy and focus to use it. It's like going on a long car journey and willingly letting someone you trust take over the wheel. Done respectfully and at the right time, it is not felt as wresting control from you but as care and support.

Part of the social worker's professionalism is the other professional contacts that it provides. 'She puts me in touch with other professionals,' notes Mrs Corbett. 'When there was all that business with the care agency, the chap who came, Richard, Harold insisted that we kept him on. Harold trusted Richard,' and the social worker battled for them so that Richard stayed. 'She was a good go-between – when Harold was in great distress with the hearing and sight problems, she put me in touch with various groups for people with sight and hearing problems. He preferred the one at the Catholic Church, there was a rugby connection and it was more Harold's type. They let me go with him the first time, just to see what was going on. The people at the church were very supportive, and they never tried to make him a Catholic!' Social workers' knowledge of their local community and the informal resources can play an important part in supporting people.

Sadly, Harold died almost a year ago. The social worker came to the funeral. 'She showed such understanding and appreciation. She treated me with respect. She was wonderful at the time of Harold's death. My brain turned to dust and she just dealt with things.' Continuity of contact is important for Mrs Corbett. Her social worker continues to have contact with her beyond these crises. 'She calls in about once a term to see how I'm getting on,' says Mrs Corbett, revealing her teacher-eye view of the passing of time. It seems that Mrs Corbett's social worker manages to combine a sense of being both good friend and sound professional.

For all the importance of the skills and the knowledge, Mrs Corbett very helpfully reminds us what is also important about social work is *how* it is done. 'She does it in such a lovely, gentle, kind way.'

What we can learn from Mrs Corbett's story

Mrs Corbett's story throws light on many different aspects of good practice. Before you read our analysis below, perhaps you would like to make a list of your own headlines. What are the important messages from your reading of Mrs Corbett's positive experience of social work?

Below we present ten themes from Mrs Corbett's story. See how they compare with your own list and with Francis and Netten's (2004) six key aspects of quality arising from their study of service users' views of home care: reliability, continuity, flexibility, communication, staff attitudes, and staff skills and knowledge.

1 Showing respect

The social worker came to the funeral.

We all have our own sense of what 'respect' means. There are perhaps some universal indicators of respect, such as listening to others' points of view and showing that these are important, even if conflicting with your own. Respectful treatment shows care for the whole person and a desire to engage with the world as they see it, even if this is difficult to comprehend. Showing respect does not mean being unassertive; it is not intended to indicate deference, for example. Indeed, we might think that respect is experienced as sincere when someone is able to own up to their disagreement with a person's views, whilst still recognising them as a person.

Sometimes a particular act can convey respect. For Mrs Corbett, the social worker's decision to come to her husband's funeral, as well as all the support she gave her around that time, sums up the respect she feels that the social worker has for her.

2 Staying calm

'She was calm about the situation. She dealt with it.'

Mrs Corbett recognises that there have been times when she and her husband were in panic – 'mad' she describes it on one occasion. At those times, she appreciated the calmness which both her social workers brought to the situation. This is not the placatory or patronising kind of calmness, in which the person is told that there is nothing to worry about; this calm is one that understands the anxiety, accepts it, but does not let it incapacitate the worker. Staying calm can be very difficult when others are highly charged, but it will give them confidence to try to find their own 'centre' in the knowledge that someone who knows them will, for now, 'deal with it'.

3 Responding quickly

'She tore through the paperwork ... she would just deal with it.'

If we think of ourselves as the users of services, we know how much we appreciate prompt and responsive action – plumbers and electricians who come when they say they will, who have the correct parts and know how to fit them. Of course, delays are sometimes unavoidable, so the plumber who rings ahead to apologise for a delay and to give an estimated new time, or the electrician who forewarns that the necessary component may have to be ordered and gives a realistic timetable, are also seen as acting responsively and professionally. Social workers cannot react to every demand, of course; but they need to negotiate with the people they are working with about what they can each expect; and if one social worker can 'tear through the paperwork' it is reasonable to expect all social workers to be able to do much the same.

4 Keeping and letting go of control

'It's OK because I feel in charge ... at one point she took over marvellously.'

Common to all our stories is the question of control – who has it when, how is it kept, shared and released. We have already seen in Humerah's story (Chapter 2) that a naive interpretation of control is that it is good for service users and bad for social workers and that 'empowerment' is somehow the complete relinquishment of power by social workers to service users. We hope that this stark and two-dimensional view of control has disappeared, not least because social workers have powers which they cannot disown, and service users know this.

Mrs Corbett illustrates the way in which control needs to be fluid, to ebb and flow. At one point she says how everything was OK because she felt in charge of what was happening (the decision to use a particular care agency, for example); at another she praises the way in which the social worker was able to take over – 'marvellously'. Mrs Corbett sees no paradox here because the social workers were able to respond to different circumstances at different times. Had the social workers taken their cue from an ideological definition of empowerment they may have been less successful, but they were able to respond to what Mr and Mrs Corbett wanted and needed and the evidence for this is Mrs Corbett's obvious satisfaction with the experience over time.

5 Recognising and anticipating feelings

'I was feeling terribly vulnerable ...'
'She could anticipate if Harry was getting over-anxious'

We have noted elsewhere (Doel, 2006) the value of responding to feelings in groupwork, and Mrs Corbett's narrative suggests the same is true in individual work. The current focus on outcomes can sometimes lead to the neglect of the processes that lead to successful results. Mrs Corbett's experience also seems to suggest that it is important to *anticipate* feelings, such as the signs that Harold's anxiety was building. How did the social workers do this? In the absence of the workers' stories, we can only make inferences. Perhaps it is a combination of their specific knowledge of Mr and Mrs Corbett, and their general knowledge of people in this kind of situation (in French, a combination of *connaisser* and *savoir*) which led to their ability to anticipate, and to do this successfully.

It is interesting to speculate on the proportion of these two kinds of knowledge. The reliance on generalised knowledge is perhaps stronger than we are aware – the tendency to look for characteristics that confirm rather than cast doubt on our beliefs. For example, which believer in the anticipatory power of astrology remarks, 'That's extraordinary, you're a Virgoan yet don't act a bit like one; maybe I'll have to reconsider!'? There are many generalised models in the social and psychological sciences, such as the stages of grieving, but how reliable are they for anticipating the feelings that Mrs Corbett, specifically, will experience? To what extent might we actively look for behaviour which challenges our belief in a particular model of the stages of grief?

We suspect that Mrs Corbett's social workers had a very keen sense of observation and, in getting to know Mr Corbett over a period of time, were able to use their experience of his specific past patterns to antici-pate possible future ones. If this is correct, we might add the power of observation to our lengthening list of social worker skills.

6 Creating choice

'That group was more Harry's type.'

Choice is a highly politicised notion. In particular, in the discourse of health and social care in the UK, choice is as a way of generating effec-tive competition, of stimulating variety, an expression of consumer rights, the fragmentation into two tier (and more) provision, and as only really meaningful to those with purchasing power. However, the idea of choice needs to be reclaimed, because the ability to make choices and to have these acted upon is central to positive social working.

Mrs Corbett is very clear throughout her story about the kinds of choices that she and her husband wanted to make. Of course, they would not have chosen to need help and support; they accepted that they had no choice about that. However, once helped through this psychological barrier, the social workers made them aware of the range of provision that was available; the Corbetts were keen to exercise choice and they saw their social worker as someone to support them in making these choices. The choice of the group at the Catholic day centre is a good exam-ple of this. The Corbetts' antennae were keen about the possibility that there might be strings attached, but once they were confident that they would be accepted for their own beliefs and not pressured to change, Mr Corbett felt at home in this particular group and he made his choice.

7 Networking and planning

'She was a great go-between.'

One of the ways in which the social workers aided the Corbetts to make the choices mentioned in the previous section was to alert them to what was possible. Mrs Corbett is clear that she sees her social workers as resourceful. They know about the community and what it has to offer; they know how to deal with paperwork; they liaise with other professionals. In the language of home improvement, they 'project manage'. It is they who keep all the other workers on board, who ensure people are coming and going at the right time and are sharing the right information with the right people (and not sharing it when appropriate). Sometimes the social worker will need to advocate for the Corbetts, stand up for them and push for certain resources which are proving difficult to obtain. Of course, they will not always be successful, but they do know what is needed and wanted and they know how to go about achieving this.

8 Cultivating curiosity about the whole person

'She knew he was an intelligent man.'

It is apparent from Mrs Corbett's story that her social workers found time to get to know her and her husband beyond the 'service user', beyond people in need of support. They listened when the Corbetts spoke about their lives, they looked at photographs of them in their earlier years and in different roles, and they asked questions about their lives which went beyond the assessment schedule they would be required to complete for social services. This takes a little extra time, but not a lot. The added value in terms of the working relationship is hard to quantify; to be seen in context, past and present, and to have the curiosity of someone else about your whole life and not just the problematic part that brings them into your room, is very valuable.

Like the disabled woman who kept a photograph of herself in her graduation robes at her hospital bed to demonstrate to the traffic of staff that she was much more than her disability, it is important to Mrs Corbett that the workers appreciate her and her husband as people who are more than the sum of their needs and disabilities; people with a history as well as a present.

9 Self-disclosing

'The social workers had experienced unhappiness themselves ...'
'She would say "Oh, this is a load of rubbish!" when something just wasn't right.'

In the previous section we discussed the importance of the social workers getting to know the Corbetts as people, not just as users of their services.

This is a two-way street; Mrs Corbett also valued getting to know her social workers. They both felt able to share some darker sides of their lives with her. Quite rightly, she respects their confidence and goes no further than to say that she knows they had their own unhappinesses. She reflects and concludes that unhappiness can have different effects on character and that in both her social workers' cases 'it had helped them to become people who give, rather than making them bitter or disappointed'.

It is clear that Mrs Corbett does not feel burdened by whatever her social workers chose to share with her; far from it, they opened a door which deepened her understanding of them, their motivations and inspirations. Dilemmas around self-disclosure are not new (Anderson and Mandell, 1989) and each social worker must make choices about how much they wish to disclose about themselves and when. Evidence is difficult to cite, but it seems likely that the trend has been to a more defensive kind of practice, so it is pleasing that these social workers felt able to buck this trend. It is perhaps no coincidence that these two social workers took the risk of self-disclosure and that they were viewed so positively by the service user.

Mrs Corbett also remarks on her first social worker's candour, which is another form of self-disclosure. The precise circumstances of remarks such as 'this is rubbish' are not known to us, but they convey a sense of a no-nonsense practitioner and one who speaks her mind when a service is not acceptable. This does not come over as disloyalty (it is probable that Mrs Corbett would not have liked that) – so it is very different from a social worker who blames his agency for things that do not happen according to plan, or bemoans her lack of power in the organisation, or suggests that previous workers were not doing their job. It suggests a social worker who is prepared to stand by her sense of what is right and what is wrong and who has the confidence to speak out about the nakedness of the 'Emperor's New Clothes'. There are times for every social worker when a decision has to be taken about whether and how to challenge the status quo, and to speak out. Service users will be watching them very carefully.

10 Maintaining continuity

'She calls in about once a term to see how I'm getting on.'

Mrs Corbett lives in a large, busy city in which we can reasonably assume the social workers are kept well occupied. Yet they are able to maintain sufficient contact with Mrs Corbett that she feels they are 'there'. It is as though they are the social equivalent of a GP – a social practitioner who has a background presence even when not actively involved.

Of course, work should not drift and there is plenty of evidence for the efficacy of 'short, fat interventions' which are time-limited (Doel and Marsh, 1992). Nevertheless, these relatively short-term encounters can be set in the context of a longer-term engagement with the community. Community social working allows for the flexible and speedy change of gear that is often necessary as people's circumstances change. Prior knowledge and low-level ongoing contact such as that described by Mrs Corbett, helps the social worker to keep a finger on the community's pulse and to anticipate possible hot spots.

What also interests about Mrs Corbett's testimony is that she has had very positive experiences with *both* her past and current social workers. Indeed, there seems to have been a sense of continuity between the two of them; though they undoubtedly had their own personal styles and characteristics, the ten themes that we have outlined above apply to both of these workers. Mrs Corbett seems to have benefited from a positive *service*, not just from positive social workers.

Summary of learning points from Mrs Corbett's story

1 Showing respect
2 Staying calm
3 Responding quickly
4 Keeping and letting go of control
5 Recognising and anticipating feelings
6 Creating choice
7 Networking and planning
8 Cultivating curiosity about the whole person
9 Self-disclosing
10 Maintaining continuity

5 Learning from Nina

'Even in really bad rain she'd come here to do the forms'

Nina is a Pakistani woman living in a council house on the outskirts of the town with her four children: three daughters, aged 16, 15 and 3, and a baby son, aged 8 months. She has been living in her current house for only four weeks and still needs some furniture. She and her husband are living separately, though his flat is not far away and he calls round most days. Nina describes their separation as amicable, but spends quite a lot of time talking about her husband and the impact of his difficult mental health on her life.

Her husband has long-standing mental health problems which have resulted in him being hospitalised under Section 3 of the Mental Health Act. She has left him and rejoined him on many occasions during their 18-year marriage. 'I left him because he went crazy and it was dangerous. It was just too much.' Her husband argued with the neighbours who lived below them in their previous flat and, despite the fact that there was no violence involved, he received a three-month prison sentence, reduced to four weeks on appeal. He was moved straight from prison to mental hospital. This was an especially stressful time for Nina, supporting her husband in prison at the same time as being pregnant with Ali, and it was a difficult pregnancy. She describes Ali as weighing just three pounds at birth and, though they shaved his head after birth according to Muslim tradition, he was not circumcised because he was considered too frail. He is now crawling and half-walking. He is quite a bonny baby, and it is difficult to imagine that he had such an uneasy start in life.

Nina continues to tell the story of her husband's illness. 'No one realised that he was ill. But he's manic depressive, that's what they've diagnosed. If he's not controlling his tablets properly he goes hyper, and when he's hyper he just talks and talks and doesn't think straight.'

Nina took him back when he came out of prison and hospital. 'I realised it wasn't his fault, that he was a person with a problem, the father of my four children – I've been with him 18 years and he's been a nice bloke.' When his parents died he had turned to drugs, largely speed, and was on these for ten years. Nina left him for five or so of those years, unable to cope with his behaviour. When he finally promised to come off the drugs and declared he wanted to be a family man and have a proper home she agreed for them to move back together. However, he suffered an intense depression, and Nina recalled walking with him to Tesco at two in the morning because he wanted to get some air but he didn't want to see people.

Nina has had contact with many services and so she is an experienced service user. She was first put in touch with the Citizens Advice Bureau by the hospital workers in connection with her financial problems. She does not read or write, so she received help with her documents. She was very sick with Ali's pregnancy and it was costing her a lot to go back and forth to the hospital, where her husband was.

Nina begins to talk about the social work student at the CAB. 'Before that there was a Pakistani man who used to come to help me with my forms and he was the one who introduced me to the student social worker. She was brilliant!' When asked to say why she was so good, Nina talks about how she did all her paperwork for her, the housing claim, income benefit, disability allowance, the lot. The moving back and forth with her husband complicated her financial situation and the student helped out with all of this. 'He'd been out of my claim and she helped me to bring him in.'

'I wouldn't have this property if not for her,' Nina states emphatically. She repeats this several times during the meeting. 'She fought with the housing people.' The Housing Department were offering Nina and her family a tenancy in a part of town where her husband's family and acquaintances lived, and Nina knew that it would be an impossible existence for them all if they were in such close proximity. 'She knew that and she fought for us. She really cared.'

When asked about the details of how she knew that she cared, Nina tells how the student would ring her up to keep her informed of news and developments. Even when there wasn't any particular news she would just give a quick call to let Nina know she was still on the case.

The student also spoke with most of the other people involved with Nina. The health visitor, the doctor, the psychiatrist, the community psychiatric nurse – she spoke with them to get evidence to build her case for Nina, and she persisted. She appealed twice. 'It couldn't have worked on that other estate. I'm on my own, my family are all in Pakistan and it just wouldn't have worked being near his family. The Housing people didn't understand. But she stuck at it with me.'

Nina recalls small details which seemed to emphasise the student's commitment to the job. 'Even in really bad rain she'd come here to do the forms.' Nina laughs as she remembers her arriving wet through because she used the buses 'and how she wouldn't even take an umbrella from me because she understood how hard life was for me'. Nina saw her as being both personable and business-like. 'It's not that she stayed long talking, you know, she'd go over the things that we needed to do, fill in forms and do what she said she would do. She'd even leave me with photocopies. I've got them all that she did for me.'

The student social worker took the time to explain things, not just the documents which Nina could not read, but also what she was doing and why, checking it out with Nina to see if that was OK. And slowly, slowly, they did begin to talk about Nina's other problems, too. So it wasn't just letters and practical things, though these were highly valued. They used to talk about Nina's problems, and the student took the trouble to spend time with her husband, too.

Nina remembers the student being with her for about six months. 'I knew that she would be there for a temporary period but I would like to show her the new house – she left before the move happened – and to thank her.'

'She'll go far,' Nina says and when pressed on this she says, 'she should be the manager, she should be the one telling people what to do.' Nina says she also liked her as a person, that she had a nice personality, but it seems to have been the way she meant business that impressed Nina the most. 'You know some people come in and they just don't look like their heart's in the job, they look tired or just not with you. That never happened with her.'

The student is certainly missed, but Nina also speaks very highly of her health visitor who has qualities which seem to be similar to the student social worker's. Nina muses that it is a matter of luck as to who you get.

Towards the end of the interview with Nina, her husband unexpectedly calls in. He talks both excitedly and depressively, and about 'big' subjects – God, philosophy, life, death. When we move the subject towards the student social worker he, too, is very positive. He says that he divides the world into the good (God) people and the bad (Dog) people, and that the student was definitely one of the good people. It is very hard for Nina's husband to focus and to be specific but he knows that 'she genuinely cared.'

What we can learn from Nina's story

Nina's story throws light on many different aspects of good practice. Before you read our commentary below, perhaps you would like to make a list of your own headlines. What are the important messages from your reading of Nina's positive experience of social work?

Below we present six themes from Nina's story. See how they compare with your own list.

1 Giving practical help

The student social worker did all the paperwork,
the housing claim, income benefit, disability allowance, the lot.

Nina is in no doubt that, without the help of the student social worker, she would not be in her present accommodation. The social worker provided a direct service for Nina, recognising the impact of the handicap of not being able to read or write. As well as being Nina's writer she also took trouble to explain what all the forms were for and what purposes they served, so that, even if Nina could not complete them herself, she was still 'the author' of the responses and she could begin to understand their significance. Nina made no reference to whether she would have liked help with her literacy, too – the student may have suggested it, we do not know. In her open conversation it is the direct assistance with the forms themselves that she most values.

It is always difficult to gauge the exent to which social workers should provide direct help – doing something for the service user rather than finding ways to help service users to do it for themselves. Usually the advice is to aim for the latter, but in what circumstances might it be right to do the former? Certainly, when there is an urgent and pressing need it would feel obstructive not to provide direct assistance. In Nina's situation, the steps that would be necessary to learn how to complete paperwork herself require medium to long-term work on her literacy. The two approaches are not mutually exclusive, so that the social worker can give direct assistance, such as completing paperwork for some one who cannot read or write, whilst considering what broader help is available to improve literacy, if that is what the person wants.

2 Advocating

The student social worker fought with the housing people.

In addition to the direct practical assistance that the student social worker provided, she went an extra mile to advocate for Nina. She made sure that she knew what Nina wanted and why, then fought hard to help her achieve it. She discovered that, though Nina wanted council accommodation, an even greater priority was to have a property that was distant from her husband's family. In fact, the student made a judgement, too, that this was a valid and reasonable desire (something which the Housing Department did not at first consider to be a factor to be taken into account). Professionals make this kind of judgement all the time, though too often this process is implicit and unquestioned. Of course, there are circumstances when the social worker cannot advocate the service user's request. Can you think of a request that Nina might have made that, as her social worker, you would not feel able to advocate for?

The student's advocacy helped Nina to feel listened to and that the student was someone who cared about her situation and who was able to ruffle feathers in order to press her case. Although social workers spend much time in negotiation and conciliation they also have to know how to create and manage conflict when it is necessary.

3 Persisting

She appealed twice.

It is the student social worker's persistence that eventually persuaded the Housing Department that Nina's request to be accommodated at distance from her husband's family was a fair one. How far we persist depends on many factors, some external (such as the importance of the cause and the nature of the resistance) and some internal (such as our ability to recover from setbacks and our commitment to the particular plan of action). We can infer from Nina's description that the student felt that Nina's case was sound and just and that she interpreted the Housing Department's response as bureaucratic or discriminatory, or both. The student made a real connection with Nina and so felt committed to fighting Nina's corner as though it were her own. If the student had been approaching this situation as 'an official' it is unlikely that she would have disputed the decisions of fellow officials.

There are other indications of the student's persistence that are not lost on Nina. She specially mentions the student struggling on public transport through heavy rain to meet her commitments with Nina and forgoing her own needs in favour of Nina's (refusing to borrow the umbrella, which would have left Nina without one). These are small but highly significant indicators for the service user of the value that the student social worker had for their work and for the determination with which she pursued it.

4 Being both friendly and business-like

'You know some people come in and they just don't look like their heart's in the job, they look tired or just not with you. That never happened with her.'

One of the messages that regularly emerges from surveys of what service users value in social workers is reliability; they do what they say they will do. Nina is impressed with the student's business-like qualities. She is always aware of why the student is there, what they hope to achieve, how and why. So, the student is not briskly getting the job done, but is taking time to explain the whys and wherefores so that Nina has a full understanding of what is happening. The student leaves photocopies of their business with Nina – they both know that Nina cannot read these herself, but they are a record of their transactions which she can share with others (friends who can read, for example) and they are a form of accountability to Nina.

Business-like does not mean cool and distant. Indeed, Nina notes that the student social worker 'had a nice personality' and that 'she genuinely cared'. Qualities of warmth and friendliness can sit alongside those of focus and purpose; indeed, when the social worker combines this range of qualities this seems to be the most effective. We do not know from what Nina has said whether the fact that the student was a different race and religion made any kind of difference, positive or negative. However, we do know that Nina felt the genuineness of the student's concern, enjoyed her company and was witness to her efficiency and ability to focus on the work they needed to achieve together.

5 Maintaining regular contact

Even when there wasn't any particular news she would just give a quick call to let Nina know she was still on the case.

Perhaps a sign of caring is making small contacts even when there is nothing specific to make contact about. Although the role of social worker and of friend are different, maintaining regular contacts even when there is nothing particular to report helps people to feel that they are not forgotten. This can be especially significant when people are feeling anxious, so that separations from people who are important to them are more acutely felt. Of course, these small contacts have to be kept within bounds, but a brief phone call in any week when there is not personal contact can be five minutes well spent. Certainly, the evidence from Nina is that these brief interlude contacts were much appreciated and they were part of what made this student social worker 'brilliant'.

The student and Nina worked together for about six months, presumably the length of the student's placement. The student had, quite rightly, explained the timescales, so that Nina knew that she would be there for a temporary period. She muses that she would like to show the student the new house ('to thank her'), since the move happened after the student left, but Nina accepts the fact that the student's contact would be temporary. Although Nina does not mention this, perhaps the fact that the student had a clear timescale, imposed by the boundaries of the placement, was an advantage. There is evidence to suggest that agreeing deadlines to achieve goals is more effective than open-ended timescales (Marsh and Doel, 2005).

6 Seeing the individual in context

The student took the trouble to spend time with her husband, too.

The student's business-like approach did not preclude time to 'slowly, slowly, begin to talk about Nina's other problems, too'. The successful achievement of the practical tasks helped Nina and the student to develop a trusting relationship in which Nina was able to talk about some of her other problems. Most obviously, these related to her husband's mental ill-health. Social work has a strong tradition of understanding individuals in the context of their families and communities, indeed of working with and between these various systems (Heus and Pincus, 1986). This has been dulled in recent years by the strength of the specialist revival in which a social worker might see their involvement as 'childcare' or 'mental health' and, therefore, restricted to only one tight aspect of a person's life.

Nina appreciates the fact that the student takes time to find out about Nina as a whole person, not just 'someone with a literacy problem' or 'someone with accommodation needs'. The student spends time with Nina's husband, too, and no doubt pays attention to the children. This reflects the fact that Nina is not an isolated individual but a person in a wider context of family, friends and community. This has become a controversial stance, and some professionals would consider that only a 'mental health worker' should be spending time with Nina's husband. This is not a view shared by Nina or her husband, both of whom valued the fact that the student social worker saw her work as engaging with Nina's wider environment – both in the home and in the wider professional community, where Nina welcomed the student making regular contact with other professionals involved in the work. Without using these specific words, we can tentatively infer that Nina appreciates the student's holistic approach.

Summary of learning points from Nina's story

1 Giving practical help
2 Advocating

3 Persisting
4 Being both friendly and business-like
5 Maintaining regular contact
6 Seeing the individual in context

6 Learning from Leone

'You wouldn't have thought it was a children's home – it had a lounge, it had a dining room, the plates weren't green'

Home

I came from a family of four children, three girls and one boy, living in England with my mother, a black African Caribbean woman. She did not have a good relationship with my dad, who left before I was born. I was the spitting image of him and this affected her parenting of me, though I did not recognise that until I was older. There was a lot of physical abuse from my mother when I was growing up. It was scary. It was not just a smack, you are talking the belt you wear around your waist, mirrors smashed on your head. In the West Indies that was the way you chastised your children, that was the done thing, but I was the rebel and I was not going to have that. I kicked against it. Eventually I ran away from home. I ran to a friend's house and stayed there but kept going to school. I was 13.

School

School was a very safe place for me. I had good teachers and enjoyed school a lot. I would not say I was bright, all my reports said, 'Leone tries hard,' I was a tryer and although I enjoyed school, I found the academic side difficult. I just kept going. At the time I was not sure of things because as a kid at home you think it is normal, it is alright. Then you develop friendships and start chatting, 'my mum doesn't do that to me'.

I built really good relationships with some of the teachers. I told two teachers about home and they would look out for me and kind of gave me permission to offload. I was scared to get changed for PE because of the wheal marks from the belt. I refused to get changed and that became an issue at school, so I confided in my PE teacher who would then let me do games in my plimsolls or give me different things to do. I did not let them tell anybody until I came back to school having run away.

I know that it would be reported straight away these days but for me at the time it was useful because I was not ready to make the move.

I did not want to leave straight away, it had to be right for me. Now there would be family support services and family centres. I do not remember anything like that. I think if there had been those sort of services available they could have educated my mother about how to chastise and parent her children, rather than thinking, 'it's a cultural thing', I think that is how it was left, it was a cultural thing. Life could have been different, but then I do not know if I would be doing what I am doing today. It was part of my mother's culture and that was perhaps one of the reasons why people did not do anything.

My mother reported me missing to the police when I ran away. They came to the school to find out what was wrong, thinking that I was just being really naughty as my mother had said that I had 'had a strop and had not come back'. What she forgot to tell them about was the beatings but I had the wheal marks to prove it. I refused to go home and I never went back ... never. It is fine to talk about it now and every time I do it kind of reaffirms the decisions that I have made and that they were the right ones. It was a big decision.

The police came and asked me about what was going on at home. I told them and said it was what normally happened and that it could be for any little thing that did not actually suit my mother at the time. They allowed me to stay at school and contacted social services. I remember this woman in a tweed skirt and jacket with a bright red handbag, with her hair in a pony and glasses, asking me about home and if I was sure I did not want to return. She listened and found somewhere for me to go.

Placement 1

I had the opportunity to go into foster care as an emergency placement. It was a black family, the foster mother was African and he was from Barbados, and they had ten children between them. I have to say that I did not like it. Some of the children wet the bed and I was in their room, which was very smelly. They lived not too far from my school and they were a black family but it really was not right for me. When the social worker came back a week later to see how I was, I asked if I could be moved. I knew what I did not want but I was not sure what I wanted. I moved three weeks later, which felt like an eternity but at least I was happier because I was safe, I was not being hit. I was able to make some friends as well, because all her children had their own networks and that was good.

Placement 2

Then I went to a children's home. It was small with eight children living there, one of whom had a disability. I had never met a child with a disability before. He had problems moving about and his head was quite big for his body. I do know that he has died, passed away. At the time it was really unusual to have contact with a child with a disability. The home had a stable group of staff who were all permanent, no agency staff coming in and out. It had a really warm, homely feel and you would not have thought it was a children's home. It had a lounge, it had a dining room, the plates weren't green. It was home.

I was the only black child to begin with and then two other girls came in, one was black and the other dual heritage. I did not actually feel different because of my race and colour, because we were all treated the same. It was as if we were in a cocoon and because it was so safe we kind of forgot what was outside, which became an issue when I tried to get a job later. It was only then that I had to confront the discrimination in the outside world. Although the hair care was not available in the home, there were facilities outside where we were encouraged to go and that was good. There was one black member of staff and as I grew older I discovered that she knew my mother, which really took me aback. I remembered that I had known her father, who had come to help us move once. My mother moved a lot. We never stayed in one place as children because she was often not able to afford the rent.

So at the age of thirteen I went into voluntary care and after six months a full Care Order was taken out. I did not go to visit my mother but I did have telephone contact with her. I saw my younger sister very rarely and my brother only when I went to town. My mother could have taken me out of care if she had wanted to but I am stubborn and so is she so it just did not happen. Some of the other children had parents who would come to see them and that did make me feel sad but I blanked it out and got on with it. That was my survival strategy and it worked. I continued at the same school and was able to keep my circle of friends. I had the same teachers who had supported me and I stayed there until I left school.

It was a safe place where I knew I would not be hit any more. Coming home from school to my mother I always felt anxious because I did not know what I would be coming home to. I knew that I did not have that worry any more and that was the main thing. It was very big for me. I made friends and that is one of my strengths as I do not like to be on my own. At home if we were beaten we could not be seen to be protecting each other as it would mean being hit for standing up for each other. We were sent to our rooms until asked to come down. So making friends and having all those people around was really helpful. But as a kid you become naughty as well. You go in as a good girl and learn behaviours from other children, get to know how the system works and what you can get away with. We used to call it 'playing the game'.

You knew if you behaved you got nice things and if you did not they were withdrawn. The game was quite simple and I learned to be a successful child in that home. I made friends, I learned how to play the game. The game really was if you were going to be childish and silly, do that away from the staff and amongst yourselves but if you needed to be adult and grown up show that to the staff who would often tell you to 'grow up' anyway, when you were difficult or naughty. If we had all behaved at the actual stage of our development the staff just would not have been able to cope with us, I think. However, we all needed an outlet for our feelings and we set off fire alarms and had sit-ins in our bedrooms, which was great fun. I know I made the staff angry at times with my behaviour, but generally my relationships with them were good. It worked because they did not treat us in a way they would not want to be treated themselves. Avril, my key worker, would say to me, 'Leone, don't swear at me because I'm not swearing at you,' and I would think phew!

There were clear rules. For example, you had a key worker who oversaw your plans and that was the person that you asked things of, like clothes or permission for an outing. You did not just go to anyone. There were set meal times and bed times. We all thought bed time was too early but we could string it out a little by leaving our bedroom doors open and shouting to each other. I had my own bedroom, my own space, whereas at home with my family I had shared with my little sister.

I was quite a private child who pretended to be hard but I was holding many strong emotions inside me. I was angry with my mother and I often gave the staff a hellish time. The home was a safe place for me but there were times when I was angry about not being with my brother and sister and I would misbehave. My brother and sister stayed with my mother and just accepted that it was the way it was. The staff would say, 'Leone why are you doing this? You are usually so well behaved,' but actually I did not always want to be well behaved. My sadness I shared with Avril, who was a remarkable woman and one of the main reasons I came through.

Avril never let me get away with anything but even when she dished out her punishment, like being grounded, she was still warm and caring. She was in a senior position in the home and had some authority, which she used to create a culture of consistency and caring amongst the staff team. The most important thing about Avril was that she had a genuine belief that I could do well. When times were bad she would say, 'Come on Leone, you can do it.' It is quite simple really, the key to doing well, you just need someone to believe in you and Avril did that for me. She would always say that she could come on shift and have an easy life, could let us do what we wanted, but she would not let us get away with anything that would not have been allowed for her own children. She was right, she could have had an easy life and some of the staff did just that, but Avril confronted things and did not just let them go. That was the big difference. She would say no to the 'f' word and insisted that knives and forks were placed on your plate in a particular way. At home we ate with spoons ... it was the Jamaican way. We learned how to behave around the table, I got birthday cards for the first time, a birthday cake, went on holiday. I learned so many things that I had never been exposed to before. I was there for a year and a half and then I moved to another children's home that had an independence unit. The idea was to find me a placement where I could be prepared for independence.

I had four field social workers during this time. Although I did not form a close relationship with all of them, there was a social worker who really supported me when my brother died in a car accident when I was 15. She also helped me with the move to the next home, understanding the huge wrench this would be and organising a phased introduction with a longer transition period than that which had been planned. Nevertheless the move was horrible for me, despite my social worker's and Avril's efforts to make this as positive as possible.

Placement 3

The next home was in a massive Victorian house, with more children and more disruptive children. There was an older group of girls who were prostituting and many were truanting from school. However, the home was near my school, which I continued to attend and I kept my networks with friends from school and from the previous children's home. Thank goodness I was not easily led.

Avril continued to visit and remarkably for me I found Nora. This was someone who would also believe in me who was a member of staff at the new home. Nora had ginger hair and bright orange freckles, which fascinated me. She made me laugh and she was very 'mumsie'. By that I mean she was very tactile. I was not used to being cuddled and it was Nora who taught me how to give and receive cuddles. Avril would give me a gentle pat but for cuddles it was Nora. Again there was a consistent team of staff who looked after us. I remember an older woman who we called Aunty Daisy, who baked cakes.

I started off downstairs in the group home, then moved upstairs into the independence unit when I was 16, where we were taught some skills for independent living. At school I was doing well and passing my exams and from there enrolled on a college course to do the preliminary certificate in social care. I did well, with good reports from placements where I worked with adolescents. I was in the independence unit for six months and from there moved to a bedsit and continued my college course. I was 17.

Out in the world on my own

Moving was scary but I had weekly visits from my social worker and Nora and Avril, who continued to be my supporters. This helped enormously as I could rely on at least three visitors every week. I had developed a new circle of friends at college but I kept my old friends from the first children's home. A really important thing was to sustain my networks and not to be wrenched from them. These girls all had similar experiences to my own and my strongest connections were with the two black girls I had lived with during my first years in care. I managed to hold onto these and create new ones. My networks were the family I did not have.

When I branched out into the world on my own the cocoon was no longer there and I was experiencing racism and discrimination, for the first time really. I had had an experience on my first holiday with Avril in Scotland, where people came up to me and stroked my skin and hair. I did not understand why they were doing that but Avril said they had never seen anyone like me before, I was different. I think that was the first time I realised I was different. It had never been particularly obvious to me as I had lived in a mixed area and attended a mixed school, which had included a lot of Muslim girls. Living in care, in the cocoon, had not prepared me to deal with racism. I would go for jobs and I sound very white on the phone and then people would see that the face did not match their expectations from the voice that they had heard. I did eventually get a Saturday job in a clothes shop, which was offered to me permanently, but I was determined to finish my college course and so that was not an option.

I did talk to Nora about my experiences but thought she would not understand, until she shared with me that her husband was Italian and she talked about his experiences as a foreigner in England. This sharing of a part of her life experience helped a great deal.

I felt lonely sometimes but I had made friends during my course and we socialised at favourite places, Rock City for a 12-hour marathon. There were boyfriends, one who cut himself, which was scary, but I was supported by Avril and Nora to deal with that and escape from the controls he was trying to impose on me. The sustained contact with those two women was very significant. I did not think I was good looking but Avril did. She still has an awful photograph of me which she carries around in her purse, refusing to replace it even though I send her new, more recent ones. I guess that is how she always thinks of me.

Working

I passed my course and was offered a job by one of my placements, in a boy's home where I worked with some of the residential social workers who had looked after me. This felt really odd but odder still was when, as a result of a reorganisation, I ended up working where I had previously lived, the home with the independence unit. Nora had left but others were still there. I did spend quite a lot of time talking to the staff about the needs of black children in care, drawing on and sharing with them my own experiences and highlighting things I would have done differently. The children did not know I had grown up in care. I do not need to share that experience with them to get results but it helps with empathising and understanding the issues. What message does it give to that young person about me being in care in relation to other members of staff that I am working with? It puts them at a disadvantage, I think.

You need to be feeling comfortable with your own experiences and how you have lived through them and this is sometimes hard to achieve. When I worked where I had lived, I could not get beyond the independence unit without panicking and getting breathless. I had a good employer who offered counselling where I had the opportunity to talk and reflect on my experiences, including identifying something I had blocked out completely. I remembered having appendicitis, calling for help and nobody coming. It was that which was the cause of my unexplained panics. Counselling was part of how I came through and was enabled to work productively with young people.

I moved and worked in other residential homes. I wanted to make a change and give some of the children the positive experiences that I had, but did not feel that my voice was loud enough. When you are really passionate about something people can switch off. They wanted qualifications, something that would back up the views that I was expressing. That was my motivation for getting qualified, as that felt like the way to make a real difference. I gained the Diploma in Social Work.

Reflections after qualification

Mine is a successful story that is unusual for children who have grown up in the care system. Some of the children that I grew up with did not have my type of support networks and I can count on the fingers of one hand those children who made it to where I am. I have to bring it back to the children's homes and the two workers who believed that I could do something, that I could be somebody. They went the extra mile with me, beyond the service offered as standard, teaching me how to budget so that I had the skills to survive that transition to living independently. I had consistent people around me and I worked hard to keep my networks, I still do. School was important as another consistent and safe place and there was the safety of clearly set boundaries for behaviour.

I am still in contact with some of the children I have worked with and I say why not? I think endings are very important, so I never like to leave anything unfinished. My own ending with my mother was very bad and I do not want others to sustain that sort of damage. I am in contact with my mother, who now has a number of disabilities, and the child in me still wants her to change. I do beat myself up sometimes when that need appears now and again. It appears when I am caring for her. Only now is she beginning to open up and tell me about what it was like living in Britain as a single mother. She had it hard but still you do not need to beat your kids. That is something she will never admit. The child in me would like to hear that from her but I never will. That is the most painful bit, because I have come through and that would be the icing on the cake.

Leone is now a resource manager in Childrens Services.

What we can we learn from Leone's story

Leone's story throws light on many different aspects of good practice and gives insights into the experience of growing up in care. Before you read our analysis below, perhaps you would like to make a list of your own headlines. What are the important messages from your reading of Leone's positive experiences ?

Below we present 11 themes from Leone's story. See how they compare with your own list.

1 Trusting children to know themselves and their situation

'I did not want to leave straight away, it had to be right for me.'

Leone's story shows that she had purpose and insight from an early age. It is important that we take account of children's expressed views and preferences and involve them in the planning for their care. Children should be assumed to know their own minds. We as adults cannot make good decisions on behalf of children, without hearing and acting on what they have to say. Whilst not acting on known abuse would be unethical and unlawful, the social worker and the police responded to Leone's wishes when it came to home and care. She was moved from her first placement in response to her unhappiness, even though she 'did not know what she wanted' instead. In the difficult transition to the home with the independence unit, Leone's social worker was able to adjust the plans for her move, taking account of her wishes and in acknowledgement of the wrench from her first safe place.

2 Finding safe places and people

'I moved three weeks later, which felt like an eternity but at least I was happier because I was safe, I was not being hit.'

An important theme from Leone's story is her relief at 'no longer being hit'. Even in her first placement this was a positive aspect of her situation. We should never underestimate the significance of suffering abuse at the hands of an adult, in a situation where the child has so little power. Home was an unsafe place for Leone, but until she had the comparisons offered by her friends, it was somehow 'normal and alright'. A priority for positive practice must be to find safe places and people, in the care system, to enable children to heal and move forward, to leave behind the perpetual anxiety and insecurity of unpredictable violence towards them from those people who should be caring for them. Even as an adult who has made a successful life for herself, Leone talks of her longing for her mother to acknowledge her abuse of her as what would be 'the icing on the cake' of her recovery.

3 Challenging cultural stereotyping

'It was part of my mother's culture and that was perhaps one of the reasons why people did not do anything.'

Leone believes that the inaction of those who knew of her situation was due to a belief that her severe chastisement was a 'cultural thing', which warranted acceptance rather than action. Whilst culturally competent practice is positive practice, it is important that this does not become negligent practice, by accepting the unacceptable in the name of what are believed to be cultural norms. She was placed with a black family but from her story we glean that matching black children and foster families is a complex web that should take account of differences in culture, rather than simply matching skin colour.

4 Listening and responding

'I was quite a private child who pretended to be hard but I was holding many strong emotions inside me.'

This is a key social work skill, the 'bread and butter' of our trade. In the story we can see many examples of good practice where Leone was listened to. The police, teachers and the social worker listened carefully to her account of life at home and acted upon this. Avril was the listener who heard not just what Leone said but recognised the unspoken messages of distress and anger that clamoured beneath the surface. The social worker offered supportive listening when Leone's brother died. Leone describes how the counselling offered to her as a young adult helped her to reflect on her experiences and reach a positive resolution.

5 Maintaining networks

'A really important thing was to sustain my networks and not be wrenched from them.'

Throughout the story there is a recurring theme that emphasises the significance to Leone of her networks. She has pursued and maintained these vigorously for herself and she identifies this as one of her strengths. However, this was also enabled by the nature of her placements that sustained rather than broke the positive contacts that had helped her to survive. She comments that her 'networks were the family that I did not have'. The losses associated with being accommodated should not be compounded by the loss of important and supportive networks that have been built up over time. Perhaps contrary to received wisdom, Avril continued to support Leone beyond her professional involvement and still does, with her photograph of the young Leone in her purse. Leone has replicated this in her own practice with young people. Leaving Local Authority care is a time of great stress and potential loneliness. The majority of young people who leave their family home are not expecting an abrupt and final ending, where their support needs and connections with family cease. We need to find ways of addressing continuing involvement that respects professional boundaries and addresses the issue of positive endings.

6 Providing substitute care

'It worked because they did not treat us in a way they would not want to be treated themselves.'

For children who are unable to continue to live in their family home, there is a clear legal and professional duty to provide substitute care. However, as we learn from Leone's story, substitute care needs to have particular qualities in order to succeed. Leone writes about her motivation to enter social work as being partly to pass on her own positive experiences and to strive to seek improvement in services. The experiences of the care system that she describes were largely of loving, warm and homely environments, where there was clear structure and where respect and affection were offered to the children. There was always someone to talk to. Learning the rules of appropriate social behaviour was important as well, essential life skills for operating in the outside world. The physical environment is important, without the classic signs of institutionalisation, characterised in her mind as 'green plates', but containing the trappings of a family home, with a lounge and dining room and space for private time as well. Nora taught Leone about cuddles, probably pushing at her professional boundaries in so doing. There are clear lessons about the needs of black children, which Leone strove to pass on to her fellow workers in social care.

7 Promoting education

'At school I was doing well and passing my exams.'

The importance of addressing the educational needs and experiences of children in care is a strong message emerging from the story. We know too well how disadvantaged such children are and Leone remarks that she could 'count on the fingers of one hand those children who made it' to where she is. Education was a key to her own future and the lack of disruption and positive involvement of her teachers were central to her success.

8 Supporting transitions

'Moving was scary but I had weekly visits from my social worker.'

The social worker and residential social workers who recognised the stress that change brings were able to support Leone in making her moves at such a young and vulnerable age. She writes of weekly visits and of 'going the extra mile' to make sure that she learned the essential skills for life as an independent adult in the outside world. This is a time of extreme vulnerability that requires sensitive and reliable support beyond the 'cocoon' of the children's home.

9 Recognising and challenging racism

'I would go for jobs and I sound very white on the phone
and then people would see that the face did not match their expectations
from the voice that they had heard. '

Leone writes powerfully of her encounters with racism and discrimination, for which life in care had not prepared her. Clearly children need to learn the skills of challenge and survival in a potentially hostile world. We note that Nora's self-disclosure about her husband enabled

Leone to trust her as one who understood, and to explore her own experiences in a search for strategies for dealing with this.

10 Knowing yourself

'You need to be feeling comfortable with your own experiences and how you have lived through them.'

Leone has had some experience similar to those of the people she is now working with (the experience of living in care). However, she is careful about how she reveals this and sensitive to the impact her own heightened 'credibility' might have on her colleagues who cannot speak from this position. What is more significant than whether your experiences match those of the people you work with, or not, is how well you know yourself and how comfortable you are with yourself. What Leone demonstrates, as a worker this time, is the importance of knowing who you are, what your strengths are and what these strengths give to your professional practice. Having experiences that are similar to the people you are working with could just as easily be detrimental as facilitative, depending on how you use these experiences. How you use them will depend on how well you know them and have come to terms with them.

11 Believing in people

'I have to bring it back to the children's homes and the two workers who believed that I could do something, that I could be somebody.'

If Leone's story speaks to us of one thing only, it has to be the power of positive messages from others who believe in one's potential to succeed, 'to be someone'. Abused children will struggle with self-esteem and with their own identities. Entering the care system can reinforce those difficulties and children may be stigmatised because of their 'in care' status. All who believed in Leone contributed to her success. They seem to have worked from a strengths model, which emphasised her abilities, her potential and her intrinsic value as a person.

As social workers we need to hear the messages from people who use services and to incorporate their insights and perspectives into the knowledge base that informs our practice. It will enrich the way in which we work for, with and alongside service users as true partners in practice.

Summary of learning points from Leone's story

1 Trusting children to know themselves and their situation
2 Finding safe places and people
3 Challenging stereotyping
4 Listening and responding
5 Maintaining networks
6 Providing substitute care
7 Promoting education
8 Supporting transitions
9 Recognising and challenging racism
10 Knowing yourself
11 Believing in people

7 Learning from Julia

'I had heard "The day we picked you up from the social workers" story, but never anything about the night that I was born'

My early years

I have known since before I was conscious of being told, that I was adopted as a baby. I cannot remember what age I was when I was told but I feel as though I have known since before I really knew what being adopted meant. Being adopted has had a tremendous effect on my life in many ways: the way I feel about myself, my relationships with other people and most importantly, my relationships with my immediate family. I have found my journey with adoption change from being an abstract idea to becoming an intrinsic part of my identity, the coloured filter through which I view the rest of my life.

When I was 19, I decided that I wanted to find out about my biological parents. I felt that I was old enough to be able to make this choice and I thought secretly that it would somehow fill the cracks of my life, somehow complete me. In retrospect I realise that I was totally unprepared and viewed this as something on my 'Things to do before I die' list. I was a restless teenager, constantly changing things about my life, and I remember thinking that it might be fun. I sent for my birth certificate without talking to my parents (of course, I thought as most teenagers do, they would not understand). It took a while to reach me and by that time I had forgotten all about it.

On the day that it arrived, the post was late and I had gone to work as usual. When I got home there was a decidedly tense atmosphere. My mother told me in a tight voice that there was some post for me and there, in the hall, larger than life, with a big stamp saying 'Birth, Deaths and Marriages – Confidential', was my reply. Of course my parents knew what it was and since it was addressed to me, I couldn't deny knowledge of it. Then came a guilt-inducing 'chat' where I was asked what my parents had done wrong, if I was unhappy and did I know how upsetting this was for them? I tried to explain my side, saying that I was just curious and that I loved them, but the damage was done. The worst of it was that the envelope only contained a letter advising me that since I was adopted prior to 1970, I would have to contact social services to receive counselling before being given any information about my adoption. At the time I thought this was outrageous; it was my life and nobody should be able to dictate or limit my knowledge of my own history. Every non-adopted person knew where they came from, so why couldn't I?

Although relations with my parents were a little strained for a time, they had obviously discussed it and one night I came home to find some certificates on my bed. When I opened them up I found a birth certificate with my birth mother's name and an adoption certificate. I felt amazed that I had once had another name and identity that I had not known had existed before. I also felt scared, as if my life might take an unforeseen turn. I recognised that I was totally unprepared, I found my emotions overwhelming, my life had shifted slightly and there was no way to change it back. I knew then that I had done this thing on a whim, not thinking of the consequences and was glad that there were barriers in place to protect me from my impulsive self. Although the information was scant I realised that my birth mother had not lived far from where I had grown up as a child, making me wonder if I may have walked past her in the street without realising it. I thought at the time that it could not have happened, I felt as though I would have recognised her instinctively, my genetic radar would have instantly sniffed out the connection.

I remember as a child I thought that my adoption added a sense of mystery to me. I used to pretend that I was really Elvis Presley's long-lost love child or that I was the real child of someone exciting and important. My brother and I used to pretend that my mum was our nanny, just looking after us until our real parents came home. One day my mother, quite rightly, became upset by this game and made us stop playing it. I cannot remember how I felt at the time but I do know that I never stopped thinking about the mysterious stranger who was my 'real mum'.

I had an unconscious sense that my position in my family was a temporary one, one of grace and favour. I felt that if I did not behave really well I might be sent to the children's home, to the mercies of foster care. I do not think that I was ever threatened with the children's home but I think that in my child-like curiosity, the explanation I was given of what it meant to be adopted led me to associate my situation as being not too far removed from that of a foster child. I heard recently of a television presenter who was adopted as a child. He spoke of the feeling of having developed a truly independent spirit from an early age, feeling that he has had to live his life on his wits, even as a small child. I thought that it was a really good description of how an adopted child feels. The feeling of separateness is no reflection on the quality of care given as a child but you feel more of an instinctive reaction, a sense of the precarious nature of your position in the family, that somehow as the genetic link with your parents is not there, your place in the family is only there by the good grace and generosity of your parents, a position that may change at any time.

Marriage and parenthood

I never really thought about contacting my birth mother for a long while, although it was always in the back of my mind that it was something that I would definitely do, I just was not sure when. In the meantime my life progressed, I moved around a lot, restlessly, never quite at home. I finally met a wonderful man and we got married. We spent the first couple of years saving for a home and furnishing it, when we finally decided to have a baby. Within a couple of months I was pregnant and on that blissfully naive cloud of first-time motherhood, where you think that the two-minute births and instant bonding shown on television is reality and everything to do with babies sends you into a fit of cooing.

Later on in my pregnancy we went for a hospital visit and I took my mother along for the ride. There were all kinds of questions asked about hereditary illnesses, which left me feeling uncomfortable, telling some stranger in front of my mother that I did not know any hereditary details as I was adopted, as if I was somehow betraying her. Worse was to come as the hospital were pushing for a test for the potential for Downs syndrome, which included a blood test, age and family health history. I objected to taking the test and had the humiliation of the hospital phoning me at work and having a heated conversation in front of my manager and several employees, desperately trying to tell the woman on the end of the phone the many reasons I objected to the test, without discussing my adoption, something I felt was private.

As the birth of my daughter approached, my relationship with my mother took a strange and unexpected turn. We both realised that neither of us had a clue about birth. My mother of course had never experienced it, making her as much in the dark as I was. Somewhere along the way we had a temporary role reversal, my mother became more of the child and I became the grown up. It was strange and felt wrong, I wanted her to tell me what to do, how to be but we soon realised that she had also never dealt with newborn babies either. This strange set of circumstances left me feeling frightened and isolated; I realised I had never heard the story that most kids get tired of hearing, 'The night that you were born' story. I had heard 'The day we picked you up from the social workers' story but never anything about the night that I was born. As a consequence, I had no idea what to expect other than what I had read and the rather glossy puff – pant – push of the Health Visitor.

When I gave birth to my daughter I had a rather traumatic time, leading to a severe bout of post-natal depression that was to last for around one year. During that time, after the depression had been diagnosed, I began to realise that a lot of my feelings were echoes of my past, unresolved questions and feelings of abandonment. At times, I even had a strong sense of jealousy, for my daughter's undeniable genetic inheritance. She was my daughter, she would always know for better or worse where she came from. She would be able to take her position as my daughter for granted, never worry about the permanence of her place within our family and never feel a poor second. I found it hard to bond with my daughter, I felt protective of this tiny baby but at the same time I felt removed emotionally. I pretended for a long time that I felt love for her; I acted the role of a loving mother whilst feeling nothing inside. This went on until I was diagnosed with post-natal depression. I had reached the bottom of the pit and after ten months I allowed myself to feel how much I loved my daughter and it took my breath away.

I looked at my baby and suddenly realised the enormous sacrifice that my birth mother made, I knew that I could never have done the same thing. By the time that my daughter was one year old, I decided that the time was right for me to start the search for my birth mother again. I felt that now I owed her the right to know that she made a good decision, that I was alive and well, I realised that she had no way of knowing such basic information.

The search for my birth mother

I contacted my local Social Services Adoption Department and spoke to a very nice woman. I was extremely nervous when I made the first phone call, tearful even, as it felt as if I was doing something really wrong, betraying the deepest darkest secret of my parents. I remember the woman on the end of the phone being very calm and reassuring, making me feel as though I was doing no wrong, that I was allowed to be a little tearful as I was making a huge step into an emotional arena I had not visited before. She arranged for me to meet with her so that she could assess whether I was ready to take this step. I was quite nervous and felt annoyed that I was being vetted to see if I was ready to find the beginning of my life story, my story, my history. I want to say that the counselling was totally unnecessary but that would not be the truth. I had thought long and hard of the possible outcomes of trying to contact my birth mother, the emotional impact and how I would cope with another possible rejection. I had not thought of the fallout for anyone else or how all my relationships within my family would shift slightly. I also explored some of the more negative things about my relationship with my parents, things I did not enjoy thinking about or talking about. I feel grateful to my parents for their love and support, I have a fierce sense of protectiveness for them and felt that discussing their weak points with a stranger was an act of betrayal. I am not sure whether my gratitude is amplified because they took me in as their own or if I would feel like this anyway, but either way my parents are quiet, private people. Initially, I did not really benefit from the counselling as I was trying to tell the social worker what I thought she wanted to hear; worried, guilty and wanting desperately to please, I could not cope with the reality of my emotions. The social worker was patient and very non-judgemental and I found myself worrying less about how she saw me and was able to concentrate more on exploring the thoughts and feelings I had. The breakthrough of the counselling happened after a seemingly trivial spat with my father. It happened half an hour prior to a counselling session and was over a broken milk bottle. I went into the session really annoyed and irritated by this incident and the social worker sensed my mood. I was extremely reluctant to talk it over with her but she gently coaxed it out of me and we examined it and turned it over and over until it became my Pandora's box. It lifted the lid to a whole range of emotions I had not thought about. Although I found the counselling hard and uncomfortable, making me face truths that I would have quite happily ignored for the rest of my life, I found it ultimately extremely helpful. I learnt about my self and my relationship with my parents. I realised that even though my parents informed me of my adoption, it was implied through day-to-day life that it was a subject that they found too difficult to talk about. This had a tremendous effect on how I felt about trying to find out my story. I felt and still feel guilty and secretive. I still cannot discuss anything surrounding the beginning of my life freely with them, as it is still too painful for all of us. I still feel like I carry around the guilt of my father's infertility, my adoption and presence being a constant daily reminder of his perceived failure to be a 'real man'. I still feel the need to appease my parents and make everything as perfect as possible to make up for not being their own child, not being born of my mother's womb or being from my father's seed. Their barrenness still haunts me.

I had decided before I began my search in earnest that I would not rush myself, I would give myself time to adjust and reassess the situation with each new development and I gave myself permission to stop and leave it at any point. After each visit to the social worker, I would give myself a few months to let everything sink in before arranging another meeting. I found some meetings better than others. I realised that the social worker had a responsibility to protect every person in the circle but I felt overprotected at some points and it seemed a painfully slow process. Eventually, I was prepared and given the green light to start my search in earnest. The social worker had found out some more information regarding my adoption and had even found some letters from my birth mother. We had decided that I would not tell my parents anything until my birth mother had decided if she wanted to meet me.

I felt that there was no point rocking the boat for a second time unnecessarily if she did not want to. We realised that there was a possibility of my grandparents still living at the same address as was on my original birth certificate and so I went to the library and searched the local electoral documents to see if they did. When I found out that they did, I must admit to driving up and down their street a few times to see if I could see them. I did not contact them, though the temptation was great. I realised they were probably quite old by this point and I thought that the shock might kill them. The social worker and I had decided that the best thing for me to do would be to write a letter to my birth mother and she would write an introduction letter to my grandparents. I took about three months to complete my letter. I agonised over it. I wanted to say so much but realised that the less pressure I put on her, the greater the chance she would want to meet me. The letter contained an introduction and my gratefulness at her decision. I told her that I would fully understand if she did not want to meet me but would she at least send me a photo so I knew who I looked like. We sent the letter off and waited with baited breath. My social worker phoned me up about a week later to tell me that my birth mother had been in contact and she would love to meet me. We arranged it for the following week and then I realised that I would have to tell my parents.

I felt sick at the idea of telling my parents. I was making a decision that could potentially break up our relationship entirely. Throughout my counselling sessions, we had discussed the potential outcomes of this moment and I felt prepared. I realised that my mother would be the best person to tell, as my relationship with my father is sometimes difficult. I went to her house when I knew my father was out and told her that I had something to tell her but I could not find the words. She told me to go home and she would be around in a while. When she came, I took a deep breath and told her. I felt as though I was breaking her heart and the thought of that day still makes me weep. We both cried, I thought she was crying through the pain I caused her but when she had recovered slightly she told me that she was crying with relief. She said that she hoped that I would find my birth mother, as she cried every time that I had a birthday; she cried for the woman out there who was wondering if her baby was alive. She cried for the gift of having a child and grandchild. She cried for the sacrifice and she cried for her own joy created through that sacrifice. I never fully understood my mother until that day. My relationship with my mother altered and I saw the power of compassion, the depth of it and the breadth of it.

I asked my mother to tell my father, which she agreed to do. I phoned my social worker as soon as my mother left and she helped me to recover my equilibrium. I needed to speak to her, as it was essential that I spoke to someone not emotionally involved. She debriefed me, cooled me down. We spoke of my conversation with my mother and what a weight off my mind it was that she knew. We also talked about the meeting the following week. My birth mother had asked if she could bring her parents along to the meeting. I felt apprehensive but decided to allow it, in retrospect I realised that it was probably not the best decision.

On the allotted day, I went to drop my daughter off at my parents' house. The mood was tense to say the very least. My mother seemed quite anxious and my father was in a terrible mood. He was short and snappy with me, adding to the guilt and fear that I was already feeling. I promised them both that I would come straight home and tell them everything. I sensed how delicate this moment was for both of them; they seemed to assume that somehow, as this woman was back in my life, she would be claiming prior ownership on me. I wanted to relieve them of this thought but at the time I was in a hurry.

By the time I arrived at the social worker's office I was late and flustered. I didn't know what to expect. My social worker came out and told me that my birth mother, her husband and my grandparents were all in another room waiting to meet me. She told me that when I was ready she would take me into the room to meet them all. I wish now that she had insisted that I was taken to see my birth mother first. I remember the door opening and being greeted by four complete strangers. They were crying and emotional, trying to hold me and kiss me. I felt nothing, no recognition, no sense of belonging. An empty attic.

I wanted to leave as soon as I had arrived, like a child receiving the toy they had been dreaming about, only to realise that they really wanted something else. I wanted to run and hide from these strange people claiming me. I did not run, good manners made me stay, answering their questions, smiling as though it was the best day of my life, being the girl I thought they wanted me to be. After a while they invited me out to lunch. The social worker told me that I did not have to go but as there were four of them and two of us, it seemed like the best thing to do. We went for lunch and during the lunch we swapped details about ourselves, likes and dislikes, what we ate, what we drank, things inconsequential. My birth mother had told me that I had two other siblings and showed me photographs of them; I showed her a photograph of my daughter. My grandparents claimed to see similarities between my birth mother and myself but I could not see it. I thought that they were extremely nice people, we shared a similar sense of humour but they did not feel related to me. I did not feel related to them. It felt as if my relatives had not turned up and the social worker had pulled four strangers off the street and paid them to pretend to be my relatives.

We parted on good terms and agreed to meet up again. As I left my birth mother hugged me and told me she loved me. That left me feeling cold and angry, she did not love me, she loved the baby she left in the Social Services office all those years ago, not me, she did not know me. I did not want her to love me.

When I got home things became even more confusing. I saw my father on the drive of his house and asked him if mother was in. He said mother's name and asked me if I meant her or my proper mother? My real mother? I cannot tell you how that felt, to think that they thought I would be so fickle as to change my parentage on the basis of this meeting, that all they had done for me was so easily undone. I went home and cried. I could not tell them how I felt verbally as it was too hard so I wrote them a letter. I told them that I loved them both and that there was only room for one mother and father in my life. I told them that they were my parents no matter who came along, they picked me up when I fell, gave me shoulders to cry on when things got tough and taught me the lessons in life that only a parent can. They earned their badge of mother and father. It was a badge for life and was accompanied with a badge of honour for grandparents. They had nothing to fear. I took the letter around to them. There were many tears. My mother still has the letter.

What worked for me

After I got home that evening, I phoned my social worker. We talked about what had happened and she debriefed me. I cannot remember if I saw her again or talked to her at all but I am sure I did. I found the Social Services a tremendous help. They reassured me in my darkest moments and allowed me the freedom to explore the complex emotions surrounding this part of my life. I would have liked to have changed two things. I feel that the meeting with my birth mother and her parents would have been better for me if it was just between myself and my birth mother. I felt sorry for my social worker as she was ambushed by my grandparents and my birth mother's husband. I feel that there must be a proportional representation in the room at a meeting such as this. There seemed to be so many people in that room and the only person I wanted to meet was being over-shadowed. I felt outnumbered and I feel that the social worker was outnumbered too.

The second would be that my parents received counselling as well. There should be a time of grace in between the moment when a birth parent has agreed to meet and the adoptive parents have been told of the meeting, where counselling is arranged for the adoptive parents to allow them to sort through their feelings. Even if the offer of counselling is not taken up, at least they would have the chance to talk to someone who knows the adoptee and their motives and can reassure the adoptive parents. I felt that my parents were left high and dry. I know that

I am speaking as a layperson, but I feel my parents were the only people who were not taken care of.

The ending of the story

To round off the tale, I did meet several times with my birth mother but felt that she was ambiguous in her feelings towards me. She told me on more than one occasion that she felt little for me and thought more of my daughter than she did of me. I felt as if she seemed to have little regard for my feelings, as if she was waiting for the axe to fall and when it did not, when I did not rant or rave at her, she wanted to provoke a reaction out of me by being heartless. She also told me that she had a bus accident when she was three months pregnant 'and you still didn't shift'. I did not feel hurt by this comment but thought that if I carried on the relationship and invested more emotion into it, her lack of regard for my feelings could really hurt me. The good news is that I do regularly see my grandparents. They have welcomed me into their lives with open arms and now, through the course of time, I have grown to love them. I understand the unconditional bit now. I think that my relationship with them is made easier by the fact that my parents know that I see them regularly and since I have no surviving adopted grandparents, I do not feel as if I am betraying anyone.

The journey that I took was a long and hard one. I am still not sure that I got what I wanted at the beginning of my journey, but what I do have now, I would not swap.

What we can learn from Julia's story

Julia's story throws light on many different aspects of good practice and gives insights into the experience of adoption. Before you read our analysis below, perhaps you would like to make a list of your own headlines. What are the important messages from your reading of Julia's experiences?

Below we present eight themes from Julia's story. See how they compare with your own list.

1 Understanding the significance of adoption for identity formation

'I have found my journey with adoption change from being an abstract idea to becoming an intrinsic part of my identity, the coloured filter through which I view the rest of my life.'

Julia's story speaks powerfully to us of her life growing up as an adopted child and the significance of this in adulthood, particularly when she became a parent. We can learn from her about her feelings of insecurity because of her perceived sense of the 'precarious nature of her position in the family'. If you can be taken in, surely you can be given back. We learn how she fantasised about her origins, how she felt she needed to earn her place in the family, 'making everything as perfect as possible'.

2 Knowing the law and your statutory responsibilities

'The worst of it was that the envelope only contained a letter advising me that I would have to contact social services to receive counselling before being given any information about my adoption.'

Julia was obliged to agree to counselling before she was able to contact her birth parents. As social workers we must work within the legal framework and discharge our responsibilities in line with this. The social worker was knowledgeable about adoption law and the process moved smoothly, if a little slowly at times for Julia, within the legal framework.

3 Recognising and responding to emotions

'I remember the woman on the end of the phone being very calm and reassuring, making me feel as though I was doing no wrong.'

Julia's story overflows with strong, shifting and at times contradictory emotions. At various points Julia writes of her emotions overwhelming her. During counselling she showed anger, guilt, deeply rooted grief, betrayal, emptiness and disappointment, to name but a few. Julia's social worker seems to have been very skilled in this area, including helping Julia to explore anticipated emotions as a rehearsal for the events that would challenge her greatly. Whilst Julia was initially resentful about the process, 'it was my life,' it ultimately enabled her to face difficult truths and to 'explore the complex emotions surrounding this part of my life'.

4 Being non-judgemental

'They reassured me in my darkest moments and allowed me to explore the complex emotions surrounding this part of my life.'

Julia's story highlights this characteristic as being a particularly positive aspect of the social worker. She needed to be able to explore issues and feelings with honesty, confronting difficult emotions, 'taking a huge step into an emotional arena I had not visited before'. She describes how she was able to move from wanting to please the social worker, saying the right thing, to a position where she was freed up to talk frankly, knowing she would not be judged. It is perhaps a testimony to the depth of Julia's development that she writes so openly and with such a sense of calm about the ultimate rejection by her birth mother.

5 Offering an external perspective

'I needed to speak to her, as it was essential that I spoke to someone not emotionally involved.'

Given the strength of the emotions assailing her, Julia writes of valuing the social worker's external perspective on the situation. She needed someone who was not emotionally involved, someone who could be calming and reassuring in the face of her turmoil. From Julia's account it is difficult to imagine that the social worker was not emotionally moved by her story and we do form connections with the people that we work with. We could speculate that the social worker was able to manage her feelings, demonstrate warmth and connectivity whilst offering a positive and professional service.

6 Being a conduit between people

'The social worker had found out some more information regarding my adoption and had even found some letters from my birth mother.'

Julia's social worker was initially the link between Julia and her birth family. She had the task of making enquiries, offering counselling, sharing information and writing an initial letter of introduction to Julia's birth mother. Whilst this is a legal requirement, it was important to manage this effectively for Julia and for the other people involved in the situation. It will have required the skills of liaising, presenting choices and ensuring the boundaries of confidentiality were clear.

Julia's account of her first meeting with her birth family demonstrates the importance of having a known and trusted ally as both a supporter and as someone who will ease communication between 'strangers' in an emotionally charged situation. Julia's reflections about feeling 'ambushed' and overwhelmed by the presence of so many people in the room offers us learning about managing encounters and addressing power issues in interactions.

7 Being sensitive to the person's own pace

'It took about three months to complete my letter. I agonised over it.'

Julia, whilst initially frustrated by the need for a legal and administrative process, describes how pleased she was that there were 'barriers in place to protect me from my impulsive self'. When she eventually began her search in earnest she writes of giving herself 'permission' to stop at any point and of meetings that were arranged to her own timescales, not set by the social worker or the demands of any legal process. Whilst this cannot be the case in all situations, for example child protection contexts, it was clearly important that Julia was steering this process. This was linked to her emotional need to 'adjust and reassess the situation with each new development'.

8 Recognising the needs of others

'I know that I am speaking as a layperson, but I feel my [adoptive] parents were the only people who were not taken care of.'

Social workers need to be clear about the boundaries of their roles and purpose. We can find ourselves in situations where we are involved with a range of people, often with complex and competing needs and perspectives. For people to be clear about what can be offered and for ourselves to be able to manage complex situations, we need to be able to answer the question, 'who am I here for and why?'

Julia has identified in her account what she believes to be the unmet needs of her adoptive parents. She chronicles the significance of the counselling for her own development and survival and sees the gap for her adoptive parents, whose emotions were also both complex and strong. Social workers can have a role in identifying gaps in provision and in lobbying for the development of services to ensure they respond appropriately to all the needs.

Summary of learning points from Julia's story

1 Understanding the significance of adoption for identity formation
2 Knowing the law and your statutory responsibilities
3 Recognising and responding to emotions
4 Being non-judgemental
5 Offering an external perspective
6 Being a conduit between people
7 Being sensitive to the person's own pace
8 Recognising the needs of others

8 Learning from John

'I instantly felt as though I was being listened to and that I had a chance of being seen as normal'

Context: the Early Intervention in Psychosis Service

The Early Intervention in Psychosis Service (EI) provides a three-year social and health care service for young people between 14 and 35 years of age. Early intervention in psychosis 'amounts to deciding if a psychotic disorder has commenced and then offering effective intervention at the earliest possible point and secondly, ensuring that intervention constitutes best practice for this phase of illness, and is not just the translation of standard treatments developed for later stages of need' (McGorry 2005: 305).

The team consists of social workers, nurses, psychiatrists and psychologists. The team ethos is to engage with young people in assertive and creative ways, treat the symptoms of psychosis as early as possible, and work jointly with service users and their families towards recovery and brighter futures. The team works hard to promote a philosophy of 'normalising' mental health care in the community, breaking down stigma and reducing disadvantage. The approaches used to achieve this are simple but effective. For instance, the service plants itself within schools, local surgeries and Jobcentres. The service has a local agreement with the YMCA, Prince's Trust and FE College. Indeed, an EI 'Job Club' has helped forge a union between service users and local commercial business. Therefore, using the community as a resource helps reduce social exclusion, tackle unemployment and combat stigma.

After three years of operation the service has seen 62% of service users return to work or education, experience reduced symptoms of psychosis and improve their relationships with families and their peer group. The aim of the service is to make a genuine difference to service users' experiences of the mental health care system. The vision of the service is to change both individuals' lives and the public perception of mental ill health.

John is a young man who has had support from his social worker, Mike, for three years, through his early experience of psychosis and in his journey to recovery. John's thoughts and feelings are told in his own words. His story focuses on mometous changes – in his own life, the attitudes of his family and the perception of his employers. Young adults with mental health problems are one of the most excluded groups in society. The story has a focus not only on recovery from mental ill health but also on gaining employment as a person with a severe mental health problem. This emerges as key to breaking the cycle of disadvantage.

A recent government report[1] highlighted stigma and the resulting discrimination as the greatest barriers to social inclusion for people with severe mental illness. Without a significant shift in the way our society responds to mental health issues the government's aspirations of tackling social exclusion will be hard to realise. John's story tells of how families, employers and local communities each have a role to play in fuelling this stigma. For example, the drive to move off sickness benefit and into employment has created an increased anxiety in John's recovery. In addition, the media have a role in fuelling stigma towards people with mental health problems. Forty per cent of the public associate mental illness with violence (Glasgow Media Group, 1994). How do we ensure a significant shift in the way our society responds, to positively promote mental health issues?

John's story illustrates how, when agencies combine their expertise and work in partnership, they can truly shape the essence of social and health care. This involves ensuring that people using services have genuine choices and can take control of their own circumstances. It means maximising people's life chances and delivering integrated care to meet their health and social care needs.

John

At school I was not fantastic. Indeed I always stood out and I stood out because I had dyslexia. I found it difficult to build relationships with friends but I worked hard on my relationships with staff and teachers. I think I did this because I knew I always struggled academically and if

---

[1] This report was titled *Mental Health and Social Exclusion* and was published by the Social Exclusion Unit in 2004. The Unit has since closed but the report is available from http://archive.cabinetoffice.gov.uk

they saw me making an extra effort this would in some way help me to achieve good grades. I first had contact with mental health services when I was ten or eleven. I had high levels of anxiety and I was seeing 'little green men'. I saw a psychologist for this problem on more than two occasions, but after time and stress levels going down this seemed to resolve itself. When I look back I realise this was around the time my parents told me they were going to split up. My relationship with my mother was very difficult from then on, it still is now.

Throughout my school life I was told I was not going to achieve any GCSEs. I suppose looking back I always wanted to fight against the negative image that people had of me. Throughout my teens I struggled with dyslexia, I struggled with anxiety and I struggled with my eating. Indeed my eating was so bad I used to vomit before or after dinner, such was my anxiety and nervous tension. I had some learning support from my local school that helped me a lot. I always seemed to be struggling with shaking off the belief of people who thought I was different, odd or not quite hitting the mark. However, I successfully passed my GCSEs much to my own satisfaction and amazement.

I left the college in the neighbouring town at the age of 16 to pursue a course in theatrical lighting that was of particular interest to me. I feel in some ways this gave me the real turning point to reinvent myself. Looking back now on the work I did with my social worker, Mike, I realise that in some way this was about taking charge of my life story, because up until then everybody had pretty much written it for me, that I wasn't going to go anywhere, that I was always going to struggle. However, I am glad to look back and say I really proved this to be wrong. I reinvented myself and then I went to attend drama school in London. Shortly before starting drama school I won a stage award in 2004 and my work was rated by *The Sunday Times*. I went to Edinburgh for two months then arranged to go to college in London to study lighting and design. That summer proved difficult for me. I was working long hours, I was missing a lot of food and my relationships began to struggle.

My experience of psychosis

I began to feel alone, I became very emotional and when I left for London, within the first week I realised that things were more than not right, in fact they were quite scary because I started seeing thoughts laid out before me. I imagined that I was watching videos on the television and that I was actually part of them and that I was able to see people's conversations around me. In fact I recalled quite vivid images of my youth and childhood and they became more intrusive as the days and the weeks went by. I came back to my home and lived with my stepmother and my father. My family noticed that my sleep was becoming disturbed, apparently I had insomnia and I knew that I was spending many hours lying awake at night with racing thoughts.

I was preoccupied, particularly with feeling guilty. I talked on many occasions about feeling like my life was a joke. The way I felt was not like a wound that was caused by a cut, it was something more internal, more in my mind, deeper and harder to fix. I knew that I struggled with my self-identity and I struggled with these thoughts and I struggled with low energy, real dark feeling of mood. I couldn't watch the television properly without believing it was talking about me. I was diagnosed as being depressed and anorexic. I had impaired concentration according to the GP and I couldn't organise my own thoughts. My GP described my thoughts as auditory hallucinations consisting of two voices, one male, one female, which typically commented on me and talked nonsense. The truth of the matter was this jargon was actually very accurate, it was a very clear reflection of what I was experiencing and was very scary. On further talking to my GP I was referred to the local Community Mental Health Team. I realised then I had become a 'referral', a statistic, a name on a piece of paper with a risk assessment attached.

I was referred to this mental health meeting and I recall a very tiny little room with old posters talking about schizophrenia and bi-polar affective disorder. I remember sitting next to two patients who looked disturbed, unkempt and very poorly. I was only 18 years old. I felt well out of my depth, in the wrong place, I really didn't know what life had ahead for me. I had to wait for two appointments. I saw one mental health nurse who then told me that I needed to go to another room to see a doctor. It took over an hour for me to wait between appointments. Looking back I cannot understand why I got referred to one person and referred to another person only to be told that I needed to go and see another person, all within the same building. I thought to myself, God I'm not crazy, it is this system that is crazy. So I told my story again, twice within the space of two hours, to another health professional, this time he was a doctor. He then reflected back to me and told me I had early signs of psychosis. I did not know what this meant. He told me that I was hearing voices. He told me that I could not recover without specialist help. I felt very vulnerable, in fact this was the first time that I admitted to attempting suicide. I came out of that building feeling that I was a patient, I had no control and was no longer the expert of my own body. I had to pick up a prescription for anti-psychotic medication but I did not know really what this was, nor what it would do for me, if I continued taking it until I was 50.

I had a vision about what a psychotic person was, to me it was someone who took drugs, constantly abused their body and was down and out with no home. I was referred to a team called an early intervention in psychosis team and at the same time I saw a crisis response team.

This crisis response team gave me an ultimatum of hospital or of being treated with some medication at home. I made the decision to take medication because I was too frightened to go into a hospital ward. I had visions of it being a long white corridor with people with strait-ackets and other people that seemed to be lost souls. Indeed I was too frightened of this image not to take my medication at home. At this point I met a man called Mike who was to become my social worker. I was very thankful that he came on board, along with a doctor and also my family eventually felt happy as well. My first question to Mike was, 'how long am I going to see you before you change into somebody else?' He responded to me by saying, 'it is likely that you will see me for the next three years, oh and by the way I'm not going to change into anyone else'. I realised then that not only was he friendly but also he had quite a good sense of humour. I instantly felt as though I was being listened to and that I had a chance of being seen as normal.

Mike worked for the early intervention psychosis team and in the early days we simply got to know each other by talking about my experiences over the years. We talked about my life growing up as a child, we talked about my experience of being referred by the GP into services, and the voices and visions and images I was experiencing. We also then talked about my future, what it meant for me and where I'd like to take it. He explained very clearly how recovery is very possible and how recognising my early signs of illness was crucial to my long-term recovery. Mike made the link between my GP and the specialist team seem accessible and put an end to referral upon referral, upon referral. Our work primarily consisted of short-term and long-term goal-setting, having an appreciation of my past and recent experiences in order to plan for my future. Indeed he had an understanding of my biological, my psychological and my social needs. It was not a one-dimensional view that he had, it was rather like I was a whole, complete person.

We also talked about my spiritual life, we talked about God, Christian values and the challenges that this created in life, especially when you get ploughed through the mental health system and especially when you have heard voices, seen odd images and in the worst times the television that feels as though it is talking to you. Mike helped me build a bridge really, a bridge between a rocky past, and now I am in it, a very positive future. It was not just about talking about problems, sitting back and analysing things, it was real. Goals were achievable. They were my goals, I was made to feel as though I was the expert of my own body, my own mind, and not the other way round, where it is a professional who is the expert. Although, I suppose thinking about it, maybe that was a strategy, but I'm glad it was and if it was I think it worked.

I had some psychological input as well as Mike and the consultant psychiatrist. This I found really useful but as a family we found that we needed it a lot earlier and a lot quicker and when we did receive it, it felt too late to really help us. However looking back maybe that was all about where we were as a family and perhaps it raised some hard, reflective times for us as 'a broken family unit'. I fed this back to Mike. I said, 'the family work would have been really useful, but much earlier on'. I do believe that the local service will take these views on board. In fact I know they have. There again I feel confident that the early intervention service really truly did, does and will listen to service users and our families. Mike advocated family work. I didn't really listen, it did not really mean much to me but I do, looking back, really appreciate how it would help others.

My journey to recovery via public services

For two years I spent time getting used to my life in public services, not working, never thinking about my future. I spent time talking with a student social worker called Laura. I knew that she talked a lot with Mike and my psychiatrist. In fact looking back, all of their work and conversations were so joined up, they all seemed to know what the plan was for me and they all seemed to know how I wanted things to be done and they all seemed to work together.

I used to take the student social worker, Laura, for long walks in the muddy fields at the back of my house. I enjoyed these times, it helped me reflect, it helped me plan and it helped me talk which was something I wasn't used to doing. It was self-esteem, self-worth, self-confidence which were the three key areas that were being worked on, though I didn't really appreciate that at the time. I got to a point where I started getting used to my medication and felt the positive effects that it was giving me. I started forming my beliefs and my thoughts and I started to realise that I could actually make a change and make a difference to my life. I applied for a job in central London working in a sound production and lighting department, and I got it. I knew I was doing well because I was commuting into central London for one whole month. It was a success. Then I did have a blip because I was made redundant.

My self-confidence went down, I felt low, I felt that I needed the support of my social worker more than ever at this time. In fact I was worried that I was going to have a relapse but I didn't. I was able to recognise I needed a brief increase in my medication. I looked at my early warning signs and my need for rest, discussion and goal-planning again. To call upon my social worker, Mike, was very useful, very beneficial and we kept in regular contact, even when I was in London. This frequent contact helped me get another job in London – I've now been working for a major lighting company for nearly a year.

How my life is now

Through my time in London I have still maintained frequent contact with Mike. I now realise what makes me confident, how I can increase my self-esteem and how goal-setting and working at tasks helps me be confident. I have also become an expert, I believe, in my medication. My life I would say is now amazing, I could not ask for anything better. From knowing nobody, from high anxiety, from being in the mental health system I now have a beautiful home in a wonderful part of west London, a stable and growing social group. I have very good friends, I go out, I have girlfriends. I have no thoughts of self-harm, though I do sometimes have a wobbly sense of self-esteem.

I do go through blips but I know what a blip is, Mike and I have discussed this, it can be a brief incident of psychosis. However, I know how I can control it, I know my early warning signs and I know that I have been through these things before and I'm not prepared to let things drift too low, like I have done in the past. Sometimes I do get very low, I go through ups and downs, sometimes I feel very alone, very empty and down. Sometimes I even lie in my bedroom and turn off the lights and I do feel very emotional. I used to call Mike often but now I am able to take control for myself. I allow myself to sleep things off, I remember the confidence-building, I remember the self-esteem strategies and I know how to look towards the future.

Although I was linked with a local mental health unit down here in west London, I don't like using it at all. It seems too clinical, it seems too connected to a medical hospital and it seems to remind me of a fear that I once had and have no longer, and that was admission to a psychiatric hospital. I've had a real investment from people in the public services. I can now truly look into the future, I want to get into the property market, I want to make a real go of my lighting career, and I'd like to be able to have an influence on other young people who are in the same situation that I was about three years ago. Mike would often talk about user and family involvement within the service. Now I understand what he meant, and I would like to be involved as a volunteer or a mentor or a buddy for other young people going through the same pathway and psychotic type experience that I went through. Ultimately I'd like to be able to let them know that there is hope, there are good services in place and that my story through the help of people like Mike and the team and my psychiatrist provides an example of how new hopes can be realised.

Mike always talked about working in partnership with others and other agencies. His belief was that working with others and other teams combined specialist skills, interests and abilities and ultimately truly made a difference. I learned to use the community as a resource rather than stay within mental health services exclusively. I think that this actively helped me to make progress because it changed my view that I could get well in the community rather than be beholden to specialist mental health services. Basically I did not feel the stigma that I feared I might. Mike actually made me feel 'normal'. Mike used to use some jargon. He used to talk about 'maximising life chances'. If I am really honest it has taken me nearly three years to truly know what he meant, because now I can sit down, think and realise that my life has been truly maximised.

What we can learn from John's story

John's story throws light on many different aspects of good practice. Before you read our analysis below, perhaps you would like to make a list of your own headlines. What are the important messages from your reading of John's positive experience of social work?

1   Understanding psychosis

'The way I felt was not like a wound that was caused by a cut, it was something more internal, more in my mind, deeper and harder to fix.'

John's story offers us powerful insights into the experience of psychosis. It is a dark, frightening and confusing place where perceptions and reality are challenged. John's world was invaded by strange images, unknown voices, the television 'was talking about me'. It was a place populated by unknown others and yet desperately lonely and fraught with anxiety. There was no rest and it set him apart. Whilst he knew there was something 'more than not right', it was nevertheless his reality that he was living through, which he thought was impossible to explain to other people. His social worker's familiarity with these experiences, through professional knowledge, was reassuring for John.

2   Providing information and enabling people to take control

'I have also become an expert, I believe, in my medication.'

The picture of John, alone at 18 years old in the small room awaiting his appointment, is vivid. He sits gazing at posters with words he does not understand, 'schizophrenia and bi-polar affective disorder'. He sits in this small place which feeds into his fear of psychiatric services, the mental hospital with a 'long white corridor with people with strait-jackets'. He receives a diagnosis that he does not understand. He knows only that he is frightened.

The social worker gave clear information aimed at helping John to understand his symptoms and to recognise early warning signs. This helped John to feel confidence to begin to control his illness, rather than his illness controlling him. He talks of the vulnerability that he felt following diagnosis, the label of 'patient' attached to him and the sense that he was no longer 'the expert of my own body'. Information is power, the saying goes, and John wanted to regain expertise in his own body and mind.

Knowledge of the relevant legislation is also important information which helps people to take more control of their lives. We will see later (Section 8) that knowledge of the Disability Discrimination Act 1995 was significant in helping to make adjustments to John's employment which, in turn, helped him to succeed.

3 Responding quickly

'They came in at a critical time when I needed them most, and did not hang around waiting on referral upon referral, upon referral.'

The frustration of telling his story to various people as part of the referral process leaps from the page, to be replaced by relief at the swift response of the social worker in the early intervention service. This is a recurring theme throughout the stories, that a quick and clear response prevents people repeating their stories and reassures them.

4 Sustaining the response as a team

'They all seemed to know how I wanted things to be done and they all seemed to work together.'

Not only was the response from the social worker swift, but it was sustained over three years. During this time, although the social worker was the key person, support was also provided by a psychiatrist and, for a while, a student social worker. It also included work with people from employment services. John therefore experienced the whole *service* positively. This experience was one of consistency and reliability and of working together. A successful team respects and makes use of a range of skills and knowledge to work with people. Team members shared information about John, including passing information to outside agencies; from John's comment at the head of this section, we can speculate that this was clearly explained and agreed with him.

5 Considering the whole person, past, present and future

> 'It was not a one-dimensional view that he had, it was rather like I was a whole, complete person.'

John talks of the social worker and himself simply getting to know each other in their early discussions. These were not narrow discussions about John's symptoms and medications, but much wider ones which helped John to know himself better, and for John and his social worker to know one another. Indeed, they went beyond John as an individual to John as a person living in a community, and John with a family. The discussions were also about preferred futures as well as the troubled past and present. One has a sense of a steady pace, where self-discovery and self-reflection are part of the process of finding out. Though the response has been swift, the pace is now different – not a speedy information-gathering and assessment process but rather a meas-ured probing and free opportunity for John to talk – on long, muddy walks sometimes. There was, perhaps unusually, an opportunity for John to explore his spiritual life, a dimension that is being increasingly addressed in the social work literature, if not so frequently in practice (Jenkins, 2004).

6 Negotiating achievable goals

> 'Goals were achievable. They were my goals.'

John's experience of the service was not only about talking, it was about an active and systematic planning of his future – how to get where he wanted to be and the steps he needed to take in order to arrive there. These goals and tasks were negotiated together with the worker and tested through discussion, as ones that were achievable. As such, they helped John to take control of his own circumstances. When he experienced his 'wobbles', one of the stabilising factors was the task orientation. These were not 'things to do', pulled out of the air, but with the social worker's guidance, they were linked systematically to medium-and longer-term goals (Marsh and Doel, 2005).

7 Instilling hope to re-write life stories

> 'Looking back now at the work I did with my social worker, I am able to realise in some way this was about taking charge of my life story, because up until then everybody had pretty much written it for me.'

The despair and fear that John was experiencing when he was referred to services and the message that he received about not being able to 'recover without professional help', was replaced by feelings of hope for the future and a gradual recognition of the strengths and qualities that he possessed which could take him there. This strengths-based approach does not deny the realities of John's illness, but it avoids an emphasis on what is 'wrong'. It is not ideological, in that medication plays its part – a significant one – in his recovery, but uses a variety of approaches all designed to instill hope and confidence through increasing control and understanding. John talks about 're-inventing' himself and dispensing with the scripts that others wrote for him.

8 Using the community as a resource

'I then applied for a job in central London and I got it. I knew I was doing well because I was commuting into central London for a whole month.'

Young people with mental health difficulties are likely to feel different and apart. Partly this is because of the negative, and often fearful stereotypes that prevail about people in these circumstances. John himself expressed his fear. Partly it relates to the ways in which people imbibe social stereotypes (internalised oppression) even when they are a member of the oppressed group. John tells us of his early life, of his difficulties making friends, of his struggle against the perceptions of others that he was 'different, odd or not quite hitting the mark', of the low expectations of him.

By making links with 'ordinary' community settings and organisations, the team uses the community as a resource for its young people. John was not linked exclusively into specialist mental health services. His recovery was supported in the community, where to his surprise, 'I did not feel the stigma as I feared I might'.

The team's emphasis on inclusion in community activities, return to education or employment, can challenge and influence prevailing negative stereotypes and replace them with better understanding and greater flexibility of approach. John made adjustments to his working conditions by actively approaching Human Resources, and this enabled him to succeed in employment.[2] Community engagement as opposed to marginalisation in specialist services enabled John to 'really feel as though I have developed the tools to get on with life'. Of course, John's success was helped hugely by his commitment and talent.

[2] The Disability Discrimination Act 1995 requires employers to make reasonable adjustments to the workplace or to working conditions, in order to enable disabled people to work, identifiable mental health conditions being one of the categories of disability covered by the Act.

Summary of learning points from John's story

1   Understanding psychosis
2   Providing information and enabling people to take control
3   Responding quickly
4   Sustaining the response as a team
5   Considering the whole person, past, present and future
6   Negotiating achievable goals
7   Instilling hope to re-write life stories
8   Using the community as a resource

9 Learning from Self-Advocates

'Social workers are very much needed – desperately'

Part A: The group

'No. 44' is a Centre run by people with learning disabilities. It is part of a wider organisation that provides support, accommodation and employment for people with learning disabilities.

In a meeting at 'No. 44' with a group of services users with learning difficulties, the question was asked 'thinking about social workers and students that you have liked, what did you like about them?' One person felt that understanding was the most important thing; understand the person, what they can do, their feelings, and also an understanding of learning disability. This was likely to make a worker appear helpful and supportive.

Confidentiality came out as a strong theme in the group discussion. 'You need a safe place where you can talk about things,' said Anne. Privacy and confidentiality is especially important because the service users know one another and their lives overlap quite a lot. In these circumstances it is particularly important for people to feel confident that what they say in the confidence of a one-to-one discussion does not go further. Brian chairs the service users' forum and he states clearly, 'I chair a meeting and whatever is said stays in that room. There are rules and what is said has to stop in that room.'

Although confidentiality was seen as really important, it was recognised that social workers do need to talk to other people to be effective. What these people hoped for was a social worker who would talk to them first about what information they felt they needed to share and with whom. This is the way in which trust is developed, and being able to feel trust was something which they felt strongly about. Trust grows if people feel that the social worker is reliable. 'You need to know they will do what they say they will do. That way you get to trust them.' Brian said that there needed to be definite timescales and deadlines. Anne said that it had taken her two and a half years to begin to trust her social worker. 'They have to be willing to learn about you. It took her a while to get used to me.' The group felt that it was important to feel that the social worker was interested in you, to find out about you and then to find out a bit more.

We talked about what should happen if things don't go well. Anne was clear that you should be able to talk about difficulties together. 'We talked about it and sorted it.'

Consistency was also valued. Anne noted that she had had four social workers and that 'when I have a change I have to get used to them'.

The group talked about gender. Brian said he was disappointed that there were not many male social workers because there were things he would want to talk about to a man rather than a woman. Barry felt the same, though not as strongly as Brian, and the women agreed that there were things they would want to talk to a female worker about.

The project is popular as a placement for students, so the service users were familiar with many different students. We discussed about what kind of student would make a really good social worker. 'They'd be easy to talk to and if I had a problem I could talk to them and they'd keep it confidential,' said Anne. This question of confidentiality had raised itself again, so we asked if there was any kind of time when it would be right for the social worker to talk about something which had been said in privacy. The group was clear that social workers should talk to other people if the person was threatening to harm themselves or another person.

Barry expressed his enjoyment of activities and how much more fun it was when you *did* something with your social worker. The project had an allotment, and he liked it when a social worker or student gardened with him. 'You get to know each when you do activities together.'

After the group we moved into individual meetings, recognising that not everyone speaks easily in a group and that there may be things that people prefer to talk about outside the group. Each person chose whether to have a supporter join them in the individual sessions.

Part B: The individuals

Terri

Terri was very keen to make her contribution. The group had not been the best place for her to talk. She says that she is shy in group situations. At her request, a worker is with her during our conversation, and later, when she hears the voice of her most trusted supporter, she dispatches the worker to find her, so that she may be with her.

The importance of the worker for Terri is made very clear. Terri talks of a 'special bond' with her and how this has helped her to turn her life around.

Terri is 39 years old and has had a troubled adult life. She talks of having bottled things up: her emotions, her frustrations, her fears and of how this has led to self-destructive behaviour, including attempting suicide and encounters with the police. She is a twin and her sister died quite recently. Even though she has had little contact with her family, this was a difficult time when the support of workers in the project, her friends and having 'things to do to take it off my mind', were very helpful. In fact, having meaningful activities for people to do together was an important part of a fulfilled life.

Terri tells of a crisis which was an important turning point in her life. She had to make some tough choices at that time. For Terri taking responsibility for herself, with reliable and understanding back-up and support, was a challenge she is proud to have been able to meet. 'I used to be someone who ran away.' What has helped is having someone with whom she can talk things through.

Terri talks about what makes a good social worker. She has clearly had a range of both helpful and problematic relationships with social workers. Over the years her social workers have been varied, arrived and left at different times.

'Put people at ease before you want them to start talking to you', is her swift first comment. This brings up the issues of reviews, informed participation and confidentiality. 'Take the person to one side before reviews, give them information and find out what the person wants.' She feels that this now happens for her but remembers a time when 'I felt put on the spot in front of everybody.' That made her clam up. What she hated most was being surprised when she found out that many people knew very personal details about her life.

Also important was to have someone to talk to afterwards – a review of the review. Clearly a review can be effective if it is prepared well and there is real participation. Confidentiality should be respected and only information that needs to be known should be revealed.

As in the group discussion, confidentiality was a significant issue for Terri. She understood that there may be times when confidentiality could not be maintained, for one's own safety for example. However, her feeling of safety and trust in a relationship came from the boundaries being clearly explained and understood and these being reflected in the social worker's practice.

Terri has been in a number of different types of accommodation and is now living in a setting that offers independence with flexible support. This means that Terri is in control of when she asks for advice or assistance. 'I am more settled in myself', and she has a voluntary job and has got her confidence back. She feels she is able to keep some things private. This is important to her, as is not feeling watched and feeling safe.

As a final thought she says, 'it's important to me to have someone who can spot when I am in trouble, without me having to tell them'. A good social worker listens to what is said *and* what is not being said but is being indicated.

Anne

Anne had been active in the group discussion and was keen for her individual interview. She was very clear and purposeful in the messages she wanted to be included in the book. She also asked for Mary to be present as her supporter.

The messages come quickly, expressed with a passion that comes from her experience. She is a young woman who has experienced many challenges in her adult life. She was 19 when she was told of her diagnosis of learning difficulty and describes this revelation as one that 'knocked me back'. She tells how angry and ashamed she felt. It would seem that there was a long struggle with this unexpected label and this caused difficult emotions and behaviours. Anne has emerged with strengths and strong feelings about labels and about her rights. 'It is nothing to be ashamed of!'

She talks about a number of moves to different accommodation and experiences with a range of social workers and support workers. She is now in her own flat within a project that has 24 hour support. She can shut her own door and call on practical support when she needs it but she wants her own true space, without the presence of the support services in the building. She will be moving to her own bungalow soon.

She has had a number of social workers and is relaxed about the sometimes frequent changes. 'Social workers need to move on for all sorts of reasons. They have their own lives to lead.'

Anne is clear about what she wants from a social worker and bases this on her considerable experience. First and foremost she wants someone who will 'fight for what I want'. When asked for more details, Anne says that the best social workers are the ones that can negotiate compromises when there is conflict. The example that she gives is of the conflicts that used to arise in reviews, where her parents were present. Anne did not, as an adult, want her parents at reviews but understood they would want to know what was discussed and decided. A compromise was negotiated by her social worker that her parents would receive minutes. This soothed the situation and upheld Anne's right to choose who would come to her review.

The right of choice is very important to Anne. Her list came quickly and easily. She wants to choose not only who attends her reviews but also when they should take place. She wants a review to be about real and realistic change and above all wants to feel that she has been heard, that what she has said has been listened to and understood.

She wants a choice about who works with her, including a choice of gender, feeling that a woman social worker would be easier to talk to about personal matters. 'I don't want a social worker to shout at me,' says Anne with heartfelt passion, recalling conflicts in the past. She also talks about how important activities are, 'being busy'. One of her hopes for the future is to be able to gain paid employment.

'People can change with the right support. Everyone deserves a second chance. Don't be judgemental. I can learn. I have something to offer other people.' If a social worker can understand this they are making a good start.

Brian

Brian has had a difficult life. In addition to his difficulties with learning, his father was schizophrenic and his childhood was not happy. He remembers the help he received from his mother and his social worker in moving into his own flat. Together, they understood him and took care of him. Brian felt it was very important that social workers make time for you and, like Barry in the group discussion, he felt that having the time to do an activity was important. 'She helped me to write a letter.'

Confidence can be undermined very quickly, as happened when Brian had a care manager whom he described as strict. 'I went back into my shell again.'

Emotional support is important, too, though this might not necessarily come from the social worker. For example, Brian now works in a cafe owned by the project and receives a lot of support from the cafe manager. He is very happy there and notes that he has come a long way since he first moved into his own flat. His confidence has also increased by chairing the service users' forum, and taking part in recruitment drives for the project. It has all built up gradually. He used to find it hard to look people directly in the eye but now, with all the support he had received, he could do that.

Brian felt that student social workers made a big difference to the project. In particular the opportunity to get to know people from different cultures. He is white, as are most of his community, but an Asian student on placement had made a real difference to his understanding and he had enjoyed this.

The journey that many people have made is quite extraordinary and it is important for social workers to be able to help people to take stock of that journey and to celebrate it.

Barry and Edie

Barry and Edie decide they want to tell their stories together.

Edie talks about one of the student social workers she liked a lot: 'She joined in.' The student took part in a trip to the seaside, and she joined Edie in the allotment to help with the gardening and helped fill out various forms. Although Edie had started by talking about what she and the student had *done* together, she finishes by saying 'I could really talk to her'.

Both Barry and Edie are very connected to the project. As well as being a service user, Edie works at one of the project's shops and Barry is the janitor for the Centre in which we are meeting. He keeps it very well and, as we have been talking about what makes a good social worker, he also says what he thinks makes a good janitor! They both feel a strong loyalty to the project and they like it when student social workers share that loyalty. 'She kept in touch even after she'd left. It's really nice to see them come back and see how they're going on, asking about us and whether we're getting the funding and that kind of thing.'

Not all students or social workers are in a position to make this kind of commitment, but having some sense of connection is very important and if this can extend beyond the usual hours or the usual placement dates this is clearly very appreciated. Actually, Edie declares 'all the students are good!' She and Barry list some of the work that students have been involved with, mainly neighbourhood projects such as helping to secure multiple play surfaces in the local park, but also individual benefits such as helping with letter writing.

When Edie is asked what is her best memory of any of her social workers she says without hesitation, 'it's when she took me out on Christmas Eve and we went to see a play. Don't ask me what it was, but it were good!' Apart from this memorable shared activity, Edie said that this social worker was 'there for me, I could always talk to her, saw her regularly'.

Barry thought that social workers should think about where they should meet service users. He felt that it should be out of the office, 'In a nice atmosphere, somewhere you feel comfortable'.

Barry and Edie are having a trial living together to see if it works out. If it does, then they hope this will become permanent. Barry made the connection between their current arrangement and social workers. 'Sometimes you just can't feel comfortable with your social worker – you should be able to give it a trial run first to test the relationship. If it works out, that is fine, but if not, then you should be able to move on and change.' Edie agrees.

What if there are disagreements? What if the social worker genuinely thinks differently about your situation? 'A social worker should listen to your point of view, but should also talk to your family and your supporters. If they talk to my supporters, they might be able to put my point of view across because they might see it better.' Barry and Edie felt that social workers should, of course, be able to talk about their situations to other people if it is necessary, but they should discuss this with them [the service users] first and usually only talk to others with their permission.

In terms of what social workers should do, Barry sees them as opening doors for you. He returned to his theme in the group, that social workers need to get involved in activities and that their main job is to help service users to socialise and to get accepted into the community. 'Activities together make it enjoyable. I think it should be enjoyable, your meeting with your social worker.' Barry mentioned how boring the project's AGM [Annual General Meeting] used to be until the service users decided to do something different. They still get through the business, but it is an enjoyable experience.

David

What was most important for David was to have a social worker who would *stay*. He had no problem with starting out with his social workers, but they left too soon and too frequently, and they did not tell him that they were leaving and he did not find out where they were going on to. 'I thought they were going to stick along me and then they go.' He makes an explosive sound to emphasize the shattering he feels when this happens. 'What would make a good social worker would be if they let you know when they're leaving, to come and say goodbye and tell you where they are moving on to.'

David had failed to gain support for his care package and he felt that a good social worker would be someone who would stand up for him and fight his corner. He feels that optimistic promises can be very hurtful and that too often 'there's nothing in writing'. He needs to feel that a social worker cares about him and has a heart for him.

Bill

The most important work that a social worker did for Bill was to complete an assessment for direct payments, which came at just the right time for him and helped to transform his life. 'The assessment has to be really good to get through the panel. She went through the assessment with me, asking me what I wanted help with and how I wanted the help. She did a really good job.' Later, Bill wanted to use his direct payment to get someone from a particular agency and the social worker helped him to set that up. Listening to what is wanted and acting on that are important qualities for a social worker. Service users need guidance through complicated systems and social workers can provide the steering. 'We all need support at times,' notes Bill.

Trust is an important item for Bill. He needs to be able to trust the workers, and this includes the students at the project. The trust comes from them being reliable. Bill notes what a responsible job it is to be a social worker. Like Barry, he also enjoys activities and sees doing things together with the students and the social workers as a good way to get to know one another.

Rebekah

Rebekah is a self-confessed 'rock babe', a Motley Crew groupie. She enjoys her work at the sandwich shop owned by the project and she likes where she lives because of the support of the staff team there. However, things had until fairly recently been very difficult indeed. She had experienced emotional bullying by one of the (now ex-) members of staff at the project. The situation had got so bad that Rebekah was on Prozac.

Her social worker's support in confronting this behaviour was crucial to Rebekah. 'She helped me loads – she was there for me.' Rebekah describes how she decided to use a neutral place to talk with her social worker about the bullying, since the staff member in question was part of the team where she lived. She trusted in her social worker and this was very important, since Rebekah was placing herself in a potentially vulnerable situation. Alongside the sound support of the manager at the sandwich shop where Rebekah works, the social worker's belief in Rebekah gave her the confidence to make a formal complaint about the staff member and to follow this through. This has helped Rebekah in other ways, too. 'I used to bottle things up and then just explode, but now I'm upfront and honest.'

Commitment is important to Rebekah. She mentions with warm approval one of the social work students who said that she would like to work at the project all the time. The theme of trust is also an important one. Rebekah was bullied at school and the teachers disliked her. She reflects how long it has taken to get over all those experiences, but that she now feels she has. An important part of this process has been the reassurance that there is someone to turn to. This reassurance also comes from the staff team where she works, that there is someone there through the night. Rebekah suffered many different kinds of phobia (thunderstorms, escalators, fireworks, etc) but she manages most of them now. In this she did not turn to the social workers but she just decided to confront the phobias herself. But she is very clear about social workers: 'they are very much needed – desperately.'

What we can learn from these stories

These stories throw light on many different aspects of good practice. Before you read our analysis below, perhaps you would like to make a list of your own headlines. What are the important messages from your reading of these largely positive experiences of social work?

The group has had considerable experience of social workers and social work students, as well as support workers and other social care staff. Of course, by no means all their experiences have been positive (though the student experience was noted as virtually 100 per cent positive). So, their collective experience of social working puts them in a particularly strong position to talk about what they valued, because they can make comparisons.

These encounters throw light on many different aspects of good practice. Whilst respecting the differences from one story to another, there are also some common themes. Below we present eight themes from these stories. See how they compare with your own list.

1 Developing understanding and not being judgemental

Understand the person, what they can do, their feelings, and also an understanding of learning disability.

Social workers encounter people who, by and large, find themselves at the margins of society. Marginalisation occurs for many different reasons and social divisions can be greater in respect of some social groups than others. The term 'learning disability', like 'mental illness', is a loose categorisation covering a wide variation of circumstances. However, what all people with a learning disability are likely to experience from the broad community is misunderstanding. They may be literally misunderstood, because of different speech patterns, and they may be socially misunderstood because of responses to situations that depart from the norm.

It is not hard to explain why the people who tell their story in this chapter feel strongly about the need for social workers to *understand* them. As they made clear, this is not so narrow as linguistic understanding, and it is more about *knowing* them as individuals – how they are feeling and what they are capable of – and also knowing at a wider level about learning disabilities and social responses to them.

Mothers of children with intellectual disabilities reported feeling that their worth and character as mothers were being continually scrutinized in their encounters with professionals (Todd and Jones, 2003). The study indicated that the mothers were willing to challenge professional perspectives of their children as part-and-parcel of being a mother. However, they were much more hesitant and reluctant to raise any needs and aspirations for their own lives.

Although this term was not used in the discussion, we might say that positive social working is about being 'in tune' with someone, being able to listen to what is *not* being said as well as what is. It's what Terri refers to when she says that 'it's important to me to have someone who can spot when I am in trouble, without me having to tell them'. A good social worker listens to what is said *and* what is not being said but is being indicated. How might you tune yourself to someone and what would indicate that you were in tune?

2 Respecting confidentiality and building trust

> They wanted social workers who would talk to them first about what information they felt they needed to share and with whom.

The desire for confidentiality to be respected emerged as a strong theme across these stories. This resonates with research evidence, such as Bland et al.'s (2006) survey in an Australian study. The personal impact of the collation and sharing of information has also been well documented by Richardson (2003).

These service users recognised that there are limits to confidentiality and that some information has to be shared with other professionals, especially if a person is threatening to harm themselves or another person. However, they want social workers to include them in discussions about how this will happen and that usually they should only talk to others with their permission. What Terri hated most was being surprised when she found out that many people knew very personal details about her life. She could reason that this might (or might not) be appropriate but wanted to be included in those discussions. So, what is valued is discussion about what information should be shared, how and with whom. Of course, privacy is especially important when there are close relationships between people, perhaps because they are residents together or dependent on the carers to a considerable degree. Having your space respected – be it physical or emotional – is high on the list.

In the group discussion it was clear that respect for confidentiality helped to build trust. That trust can take a long time to develop (two and a half years in Anne's case) and may have to combat many years' experience of mistrust, as Rebekah noted. In addition to sharing control of how information will be used, the service users felt that trust can be built by doing what you say you will do and by meeting timescales and deadlines. Rebekah notes that she had trust in her social worker, because the worker had trust in her – a belief in her. This trust gave her the confidence to face a very difficult situation.

3 Joining in activities

Her best memory of any of her social workers was
'when she took me out on Christmas Eve and we went to see a play.
Don't ask me what it was, but it were good!'

Having meaningful activities for people to do together is an important part of a fulfilled life. Barry, Anne, Bill, Brian and Edie all made reference to the prospects of getting to know their social worker (and their worker getting to know them) through some kinds of activity, such as the allotment project or helping to write a letter. Although Edie had started by talking about what she and the student had *done* together, she finishes by saying 'I could really talk to her'. So working on the allotment is not an end in itself (though it is a valuable activity) but a means by which participants can feel connected to one another and see each other in a different light.

Barry expressed his enjoyment of activities and how much more fun it was when you *did* something with your social worker. He liked it when a social worker or student gardened with him. 'You get to know each other when you do activities together.' Anne notes that through activities it is possible to show that you have something to offer other people.

Although the importance of activity is relatively well documented in groupwork (Doel, 2006), it is less so in individual work. In some minds it may seem 'unprofessional', but it does offer an opportunity for people to get to know one another through a mutual task and it can show people in a different light. It might be a situation in which the worker is less accomplished and less at home than the service user, and where it is the service user who shows the worker around. For people with learning disabilities it can be especially important to have contacts that are in situations and places where they feel most at home. This is more likely to be an allotment than an office, for example.

4 Putting people at ease and making connections

'I think it should be enjoyable, your meeting with your social worker.'

It might be a radical idea, but these service users felt there was no reason why most meetings with social workers should not be enjoyable. In part this is related to the theme of the previous section (joining in activities). The activities are not just for themselves, but they are a way in which people can feel more at ease. At a time when there is evidence that boundaries between workers and service users are becoming more tightly drawn, as a result of increasing managerialism (Malin, 2000), to what extent can social workers respond to this direct message from service users?

There are different ways in which people may feel eased and it is likely to entail some preparatory work. For example, Terri feels that social workers need to talk individually with people before they go into a review, so that the social worker and the service user are rehearsed and can speak together in the review.

Barry thought that social workers should think about where they will meet service users. He felt that it should be out of the office 'in a nice atmosphere, somewhere you feel comfortable'. The Centre is a place where the people with learning disabilities feel this familiarity and support.

5 Opening doors and recognising strengths

'The social worker's main job is to help people to get accepted into the community.'

Most people whose situations lead them to encounter social workers experience social exclusion; one of the main purposes of social working is to find opportunities for social inclusion (Sheppard, 2006). Barry felt supported by his social worker who made connections between himself and the community by opening doors that would be otherwise closed. He thought the social worker's main job was to help people to socialise and to get accepted into the community.

Opening doors often entails pushing hard on them by advocating strongly for and alongside service users; first and foremost Anne wants someone who will 'fight for what I want'. At other times it might actually require a door to be closed against others involved in the service user's life. For example, Anne talked about the conflicts that used to arise in reviews where her parents were present. As an adult, she did not want her parents at reviews, but she understood they would want to know what was discussed and decided. A compromise was negotiated by her social worker that her parents would not be present at the review, but that they would receive minutes. This soothed the situation and upheld Anne's right to choose who would come to her review, to open or close the door as she saw right.

Sometimes the doors that are opened are ones of self-belief. The social worker's belief in Rebekah's strengths gave her the confidence to take an action that put her in a potentially vulnerable position. She chose to make a formal complaint against a member of staff who was bullying her and the success of this experience further boosted her confidence.

Although the service users did not themselves frame it in these terms, it is clear that they valued practice that was based on social models of support and a rights-based approach (Beresford and Branfield, 2004). It might not always be social workers who open these doors, but they have a key role in removing obstacles and promoting social inclusion at both an individual and a community level. It is important to recognize the strengths that derive from service users' mutual support.

Opening access to resources is central to good social working. The most important work that a social worker did for Bill was to complete an assessment for direct payments, which came at just the right time for him and helped to transform his life. Service users need guidance through complicated systems, learning which doors open on to which opportunity. 'We all need support at times,' notes Bill.

6 Creating choices

'If it works out, that is fine, but if not,
then you should be able to move on and change social worker.'

The notion of choice has become highly politicised and somewhat fraught. Those people who are able to articulate their own needs forcefully are most likely to be able to exercise choice (Stanley, 1999). However, like power, this does not mean that choice in itself is a bad thing, more that we must find ways to ensure equal access to choice. The people who tell their stories in this chapter have no problem with choice, indeed they want it, but they are rightly critical when it is restricted because of their relative lack of power.

As we have seen, Anne wanted to choose not only who attends her reviews but also when they should take place. She wants a review to be about real and realistic change and above all wants to feel that her choices have been heard and understood. She wants a choice about who works with her, including a choice of gender, feeling that a woman social worker would be easier to talk to about personal matters. Barry, too, raised the issue of choice of worker. 'Sometimes you just can't feel comfortable with your social worker – you should be able to give it a trial run first to test the relationship. If it works out, that is fine, but if not, then you should be able to move on and change.' This is exactly what he and Edie are doing in terms of their relationship as a couple.

Choice is related to control, a theme that has been raised in a number of other stories and one that we have learned is very complex (in particular, see Humerah's story). The people who told their stories in this chapter all have some form of learning disability and they are keen to advocate for themselves and to gain the support of their social workers in this process, so that the control that they achieve over their own lives, and therefore their degree of choice, is maximised. Perhaps the question 'in what ways is our work helping to increase the degree of choice?' is a litmus test for social workers and service users in their work together.

7 Experiencing difference

An Asian student on placement
had made a real difference to Brian's understanding.

One of the questions that relates to the issue of choice raised in the previous section is whether service users and social workers should be 'matched' and, if so, what the basis of the matching should be. Gender was raised in the group discussion, first by one of the men who was disappointed that there were not many male social workers because there were issues he would like to discuss with a man. This theme was echoed by some of the women who, likewise, felt there were concerns that they would prefer to discuss with a female social worker and would find difficult to discuss with a man. This raises the whole question of the extent to which service users have access to a team of social workers, in the way that many people can now choose whether to consult with a male or female doctor. The importance of boundary setting is always important, but especially in relationships which cross gender (Okamoto, 2003).

There are times when difference is appreciated as a positive benefit. Brian specifically welcomed the differences that the regular supply of student social workers brought to the organisation, in particular the opportunity to get to know people from different races and cultures. He is white, as are most of his community, but a south Asian student on placement had made a real difference to his understanding of a community with which he had had no previous contact. Whatever their gender, race, sexuality or age, most of the students and social workers will be different from the service users in terms of the fact that they do not have a learning disability. This difference was not mentioned in these stories because it is probably taken for granted. However, it is a common experience for social workers to feel differences in lifestyle and life opportunities from the people they work with and it is important to know what impact this has or might have on the working relationship. We have seen from some other stories that self-disclosure can contribute to a positive encounter between social workers and service users, but that this has to be handled carefully and be appropriate to the context. In what circumstances, for example, might it be appropriate to disclose hidden differences such as sexual orientation, and when might it be more appropriate not to self-disclose?

8 Managing endings and transitions

'Come and say goodbye and tell you where they are moving on to.'

What was most important for David was to have a social worker who would *stay*. He had no problem with starting out with his social workers, but they left too soon and too frequently. Anne notes that she has had four social workers, but recognised that 'social workers need to move on for all sorts of reasons. They have their own lives to lead.' The worst thing for David, though, was social workers not telling him that they were leaving so he sometimes did not know that they had left and was certainly unaware of where they were going on to.

Undoubtedly, changes in social worker make the establishment of a working relationship difficult. As we saw in the introductory chapter, children in care stressed their desire to keep a good relationship going with a social worker even when they move placement (Voice for the Child in Care, 2004). In some cases a change of social worker is inevitable (for example, if the worker moves some distance) but there are times when continuity could be possible if given more priority.

Most of the service users telling their stories in this chapter feel a strong loyalty to their Centre and they like it when social workers and students share that loyalty. 'She kept in touch even after she'd left. It's really nice to see them come back and see how they're going on, asking about us and whether we're getting the funding and that kind of thing.' Rebekah mentions with warm approval one of the social work students who said that she would like to work at the project all the time.

Even if there are strong emotions and even some recriminations, it is very important for social workers to make sure that they handle transitions carefully. Whether it is their own transition to another job, or the service user's moving on, this is a good opportunity to take stock of the work done together, to celebrate what has been achieved and to help to plan for what remains to be done. The best social working is when outgoing and incoming social workers can meet the service user together so that there is an orderly and considered transition. This is especially important when people have experienced losses and disappearances in their lives. We should remember that some, perhaps many, people do experience their encounters with social workers as positive and the 'goodbye' is a significant one.

Indeed, Rebekah is very clear about social workers: 'they are very much needed – desperately.'

Summary of learning points from the self-advocates' stories

1 Developing understanding and not being judgemental
2 Respecting confidentiality and building trust
3 Joining in activities
4 Putting people at ease and making connections
5 Opening doors and recognising strengths
6 Creating choices
7 Experiencing difference
8 Managing endings and transitions

10 Learning from Families: parents talking, children drawing

'I thought social workers took children away, but they listen ... I don't think I would have got through the last two years without them'

The school

The school is for five-to eleven-year-old children with severe emotional and behavioural difficulties. It has a large catchment area – county-wide and beyond. All children have been excluded from mainstream settings for a variety of reasons, and all have a statement of individual needs. (This is sometimes called 'statemented).' Some have been diagnosed with complex needs which may include Attention Deficit Hyperactivity Disorder (ADHD), post-traumatic stress disorder, depression, attachment disorders, categories of abuse, challenging behaviour and learning difficulties.

The school provides a therapeutic environment where children are nurtured to achieve their potential. Emotional well-being is emphasised, with commitment to a *can do* ethos. It offers a curriculum over and above the English National Curriculum, one tailored to individual needs, with a strong emphasis on behaviour, emotional literacy and learning through play and the arts. Over time, children are helped to identify their feelings and to name them, express them and deal appropriately with them. The *can do* spirit encourages children to want to succeed, because they begin to understand their own behaviour.

The children earn rewards and their successes are made visible to themselves and others. The school looks to the five outcomes of Every Child Matters (DfES, 2003) as a guide: for children to be healthy and safe, to enjoy and make a positive contribution and to achieve economic well-being. The school works in partnership with many agencies and professionals, including educational psychologists, school nurses, speech and language therapists, mental health workers and the police. Social workers tend to become involved at crisis points.

Helen

The social work contribution comes from Helen. She is a fully qualified therapist in *theraplay* and a practice teacher. Her work aims to make changes in the lives of children and families through play. Helen's professional background was in work with children in secure accommodation, where she was frustrated by a system that intervened too late with troubled youngsters, and often in a way that addressed problem behaviour in isolation from its origins. This led her to seek work in settings where earlier intervention was possible. She had noticed the prevalence of abuse and attachment difficulties in the lives of children with behaviour problems, but referral to nurseries could reinforce these attachment disorders. Children struggling in the nursery setting often signalled the start of behaviour difficulties that meant that these children were ill prepared for mainstream schooling.

Helen set up a student unit, which would build on her work with children and their families. It operated directly from the school setting and she and the head teacher collaborated to identify the purposes of the unit in terms of the school children and the learning needs of social work students. Student social workers have worked with the children and offered support to their families in their own homes, complementing the work of teaching staff. As part of her role as practice teacher Helen sought feedback from children and their families on the effects of the service on their lives. She recorded a DVD of interviews with parents and helped children to express their views through drawings. This chapter is based on 'parents talking and children drawing'.

Parents talking

There were conversations with four families. They were asked about their situation before specialist services entered their lives, the impact of these, what worked and how they would like to see services developed. They were asked specifically to comment on the contribution of the student social worker. All names are fictitious and the following extracts are written in their own words.

Family 1

Mr and Mrs Greyson talking about their grandson, Alan

Alan is five years old and presently lives with his grandparents, Mr and Mrs Greyson. He had suffered from physical and emotional abuse and neglect and was excluded from nursery provision. The family received support from a social work student, during which time they were visited weekly. Mrs Greyson tells Alan's story.

Alan was diagnosed as having an attachment disorder and emotional problems. Before he went to the special school he was a real animal, he was terrible. He had no understanding of any rules. He didn't accept anything. He didn't sleep, he wouldn't eat properly, we couldn't take him out, he was aggressive. He would bite, kick, scratch. We couldn't take him for walks. He would run off and on several occasions we have had to have the police bring him back. For me even when he went to the special school, combining a full-time job with looking after his needs was very difficult. The school would have taken Alan from 9:00 to 3:00 but he couldn't cope with that level of separation and I needed proper support for me. It was because of his attachment disorder ... he needed to be here [at home] basically.

Now I have gone part-time and am loving every minute of it and am able to get time for myself. And Alan over the past 12 months has been able to stay longer and longer at school. We both enjoy having time for ourselves. It has been very hard, especially because we had our own children early, and when Alan was forced on to us it was quite a shock. We were ready to have *our* time but basically we were starting again with a really troubled little boy. But what do you do? You get this little fellow and you have got to look after him. You've got to do the best for him.

The school has done a lot with him and slowly but surely a year has gone by. He started to get better, mostly when he started *theraplay* and nursery. The theraplay sessions did help him calm down. It helped us as well because we could talk about things and we found out we were not on our own. Then we took him to a doctor and he did suggest some tablets, though it wasn't really for Alan's condition, but helped him calm down which helped him understand himself and then it all came together. It has come together quite quickly now, after *theraplay*, going to nursery and I think the school getting to know Alan. They needed time to understand him because he was a very difficult child. He wasn't quite five and I think it was a bit of a shock for the school to have to deal with a child who was so young.

Alan has moved on in leaps and bounds. He gets on really well at school and he gets on with his peers. We can now take him out and he plays in the park with the other little boys and girls. He has learnt to swim and ride his bike, we take him on holiday, take him out anywhere really, even the supermarket which is a delight, because before we used to have to leave the shopping and walk out. We are very pleased with him. The little boy we knew was in there, just needed bringing out. He has one fantastic character, which nobody believed was there.

The school still needs help with children of Alan's age group. They had never taken in a child of Alan's age and we all knew it was a bit of an experiment. They have worked hard for Alan but I still think they need some extra provision or support with children so young, bring these little ones in and give them the proper schooling they need in the first 12 months. I still don't agree with putting a child of four or five in say with a child of six-and-a half or seven. There is a vast difference between them even though their mental age may be similar. It was very difficult because Alan was the only one there but I think the school should be accessible to all children, not just 'statemented'[1] children.

Moira was our student social worker and we found her really helpful. She helped me on many occasions when she came out and talked. She helped put me in contact with organisations that could help *me*. I still think there is not a lot of help for children who get missed out there. I feel when the social services do get brought in, it is usually at the very last minute and there are a lot of children out there still suffering. Though the preconception is that social workers will take a child away on any whim, in fact they don't. They sit and they listen and that can help tremendously. If I was asked by other families in a similar position, I would recommend that they take a student social worker, definitely.

Family 2

Melissa talking about her daughter, Ruth

Ruth is ten years old and lives with her adoptive parents. She was excluded from mainstream school at the age of six and has a diagnosis of co-morbid ADHD. The family was supported by student social workers, during which time they were visited weekly. Melissa tells Ruth's story.

Before Ruth went to the special school, life was a bit of a nightmare. She would bite, kick, scream, head butt, and made life here really difficult. The mainstream school could not cope with her and neither could the other children. There was not an improvement straight away when Ruth went to the special school, but as time went on there was a great improvement. Now she is not the same girl.

I think what helped us was the fact that what happened in school happened at home as well, and we worked with the teachers and they

---

[1] 'Statemented' refers to the process by which children are assessed as having special educational needs. This enables resources to be given to address these, such as additional help in the classroom or access to special schools.

taught us how to help Ruth. I think the play therapy and *theraplay* helped us as well. She got those through the school and it worked really well. The play therapist worked with the school and together it worked. It helped with Ruth's attachment disorder, which had meant that she could not do things with us properly. It helped her care about us more and it helped us be able to help her. Ruth now has no behaviour problems really, I'm actually going to say this, compared to what she had before. Anybody now would think she was just a basic, normal teenager. It is just her learning difficulties now that we have to help her deal with.

The kicking, the spitting, the head butting, all of them have gone. Ruth has had 'golden days' at school. She has had twelve silver days and two days where she lost it altogether since September, so for a full year she has had golden days. It's just brilliant. She was diagnosed with ADHD and through help from the school and the *theraplay* she has changed enormously. Before if you put a video in for Ruth, by the time you had switched it on she was off doing something else. She also does word searches and things like that. She is a lot calmer than she was and she'll cuddle up and have a kiss and cuddle and sit with you, whereas before she would give you a kiss and just go away. Now she's a lot more loving and just loves to have a kiss and cuddle and be happy with it.

I am married and I have a partner who can help out when Ruth gets too much, or did get too much. I could go out and he would look after the children. I think the school could help with parents who are on their own and have difficulty finding babysitters or being able to go out on their own when the children are off school. There is nowhere for children like ours to go, because they end up getting into trouble and being thrown out of clubs. If we had somewhere that understood our children's needs, that would be good and they could maybe get the information out as to where these places are.

We had the support of a student social worker and it was really good. He was ever so nice. I had already had contact with social workers, so I suppose I had the benefit of knowing what happens, as our children were adopted and I had contact with social workers before. You find a lot of people think social workers are just there to take the kids away, whereas really they are there to help you get the support you need. Something that was really helpful was being able to ask questions and find out what was going on at school. If you are not able to have regular contact with the teachers, the social worker can help you to keep in contact and find out information for you and it makes life a bit easier. I would recommend that student social workers continue to work alongside families because as a parent you can find out much more about your child than reading what is written in books or on bits of paper.

Family 3

Trisha talking about her son, William

William is ten years old and lives with his mother. He was excluded from mainstream school at the age of seven. He has a diagnosis of ADHD. The family received support from two student social workers, during which time they were visited weekly. This is Trisha and William's story.

Living with William was really frustrating. He was all over the place and very emotional. He didn't show emotions though he had them and he had a nasty temper and then he was diagnosed with ADHD. There was a lot for William to cope with because he had not been to school for a while and being the winter he had no social life. So he was losing out on his social abilities as well as education. He had tantrums like you would see in a two-year-old, but being a bit older the tantrums were a lot stronger and he didn't think, he would just throw. He had a bad habit of throwing things. He gave me a black eye the Christmas before he went to the special school. He didn't talk, he didn't seem to communicate whatsoever. His whole life was about James Bond, he had this obsession with James Bond. It was like he was trying to fill in a gap where he wasn't learning, he wasn't socialising. He was bad tempered and very emotionally messed up in the head.

For me it was very hard work, because I had not got a lot of insight into ADHD, I had no insight into why a child would be put out of school, no insight into 'statements' [1], I had never heard that word before. I was struggling with the headmaster and William was at home and really bored and fed up with his own company. And for me it was hard work, he wouldn't go to bed at a proper time.

Since going to the special school he communicates a lot better and he has calmed down a lot. Obviously his education has gone up a lot and he enjoys school. If he thinks he is going to miss his taxi, it upsets him a lot. His behaviour is 100 per cent better. If he has a wobbly, a paddy, it is a one-off now. It gives you a shock when it happens whereas before it was something that you expected constantly. It was a constant argument but he's doing really well now.

The kids could do with playschemes and things like that, and one-to-one sessions helping the children to express themselves. I found the parents support groups very good. They were supportive and it was good to learn about what the children could eat and not eat, about colours and music and doing something about the noise in the house in the morning, when the television was on too loud and all our voices were raised because we were anxious and frustrated. We were advised to put on relaxation music instead to calm us and soothe us. I learned a lot about these things. Sharing with the other parents and realising you are not on your own was important.

I had student social workers to support me as well and they certainly gave me a different outlook on social workers. I used to have nothing good to say about them until I got one from the school and I realised that they *do* help. She was very good with arranging transport and coming out here and just discussing things. If I needed anything I could ring the school at anytime and talk to her. I found them very good. I would definitely recommend them to other families. It's nice to know you have got somebody that you can talk to, that has seen your child and is based in the school.

Family 4

Jeni talking about her son, Richard

Richard is eight years old and lives with his mother, Jeni. He was excluded from mainstream school at the age of five and has a diagnosis of attachment disorder. The family were supported by four student social workers, during which time they were visited weekly.

Actually Richard was suspended for three days for beating up his headmistress. That was the way he was. There was no way we could tell what was going on with him. After that he had 16 months off school altogether until he was ready to go back to school himself. That was when he started attending the special school because he asked to go there himself. It was a total nightmare before that. When we had him at home he was very violent to all the members of the family and he was very destructive and would not do anything he was told to do.

I didn't see an improvement straight away as he found it difficult meeting new people and actually mingling with others, so the first couple of months were a bit up and down, but once the new year came in that was it and he was totally happy with what was going on around him. He did his work, integrated with all the other children, attended activities, you know horse riding, swimming and that is the sort of thing he had never done before. I had a lot of support, I attended the family groups. They gave me help about the things I should and shouldn't do.

I also had support from student social workers. They were very helpful because they were from outside the family, so it was easier for them to see what was going on. I didn't like social workers because I was brought up in care all my life, so I knew how social workers worked. I didn't really want them involved to start with but I don't think I would have got through the last two years without them. I suffer from depression and they lifted me out of that and made me see that I can get on without having to be depressed all the time. They put me in touch with other services and this was helpful because I didn't know those places were out there.

I think it would be helpful for me and my family to have services in the community for children with special needs, you know with behaviour problems and emotional problems. There are no after-school clubs, there are no cubs, or scouts and activities like that for children with Richard's needs. I feel that we should actually recognise them as normal human beings and give them the same courtesies that we give to other children and other people in the community, because they deserve it just as much as anybody else. I'd like to make one final point and that was when Richard was a baby he actually won a contract with a modelling agency and went up and did his proofs but unfortunately he was declined for the job because of his special needs. So he was discriminated against as a nine-month-old child.

Children drawing

How were the voices of the children heard? We know from the literature how the challenge of consulting and involving children is often not fully met, particularly those of a younger age, or those who have disabilities (Audit Commission, 2003; Every Disabled Child Matters, 2006; Grimshaw and Sinclair, 1997; Thomas and O'Kane, 1999). Helen worked therapeutically with the children through drawing, to explore both their experiences of their contact with the student social workers and to help them with the ending of the relationship.

The positive nature of their experiences emerge graphically from the drawings, which indicate sorrow and loss at the ending of the contact: 'I shall miss my social worker.' One of the drawings seems like a representation of a death. Drawing, whilst talking and exploring, was the method used to deal with the emotions associated with the ending of a positive relationship.

I am much happy Now Because Helen is a great Social worker i miss her

Researching outcomes

These accounts from service users demonstrate that the efforts of the school team had a positive influence on the lives of children and their families. Helen was seeking to evaluate both the impact of the overall service and, more specifically, the effectiveness of the student unit. This unit had been established to make a positive contribution to the school, the children and families that it serves, as well as to meet the needs of the student social workers.

As part of its monitoring arrangements, the school keeps a record of all violent incidents from pupils towards other pupils and staff. To this end, Helen scrutinised records over the three-year period of the student unit. This revealed that incidents of violence fell overall, particularly those directed towards staff, which declined from 395 in Year 1 to 149 in Year 3. This is a considerable achievement.

In her selection of workload for the students, Helen had identified specific children with high numbers of recorded incidents of violence towards staff and pupils. These were the children and families with whom the students were to work. They were families with complex needs, including the management of extremely challenging behaviour from their children. The parents and children were targeted for additional support from the student social workers. This support consisted of one-to-one work with children, groupwork with children or parents and family support work. Some families received a combination of these interventions, others received just one form of support.

In addition to asking for evaluations from parents and children, Helen monitored the incidence of violence recorded by the school from the children who were receiving this additional support. With one striking exception, the incidence of violence reduced significantly and was sustained beyond the period of additional support. The child for whom the intervention had least impact was a child whose parent was experiencing severe mental health problems which had a considerable impact on her parenting. During the period when a student social worker was involved with the family, the violence was reduced but rose quickly following the ending of the contact.

This small study is not intended to demonstrate in a definitive way the efficacy of social work involvement. For example, it has not been determined which type of support was most effective – one-to-one, groupwork, family work or a particular combination of these. However, it does indicate that approaches that integrate social work and educational support, and involve families of children as well as the children themselves, has a positive effect on the behaviour of troubled children. Indeed, more recent evaluations of the interventions of the latest group of students indicate similar findings. Helen reports that children are asking to see their social workers, even those who are on the child protection register and whose families have difficult relationships with the social worker from the statutory service. When asked in an ending session about her wishes, one child replied that she wanted to be a social worker.

What we can learn from these families' stories

These stories and the work of Helen and the students throw light on many aspects of good practice and give insights into the experience of living with children with emotional and behavioural disorders. Before you read our commentary below, perhaps you would like to make a list of your own headlines. What are the important messages from your reading of these stories and the work of Helen and the students? Below we present nine themes. See how they compare with your own list.

1 Being knowledgeable

'They put me in touch with other services and that was helpful because I didn't know those places were out there.'

Whilst not pretending to be experts in behaviour disorders, it is important for social workers to have a good grasp of a range of conditions and their implications. We learn from the service users' accounts how confused they felt about their children's behaviour and their diagnoses. This was heightened by the professional language of ADHD, 'statementing' and the like. William's mother talked of how she had never heard the word *statement* in this context. This made a difficult situation more so and the students' knowledge helped to demystify some of these processes.

In addition to knowledge about the behaviours, parents reveal the importance of the student social workers' knowledge of resources and access to them. They put parents in touch with community resources and arranged practical help, like transport. Parents were largely unaware of these resources, yet appreciated how significant they were.

2 Teaching skills

'They gave me help about the things I should and shouldn't do.'

Clearly these parents have been experiencing enormous difficulties in managing their children's behaviour and the impact of this on both the children and their families can be devastating. Children experience anxiety, frustration, confusion and anger, and parents are exhausted by the constant pressure, sometimes even sustaining injuries inflicted by their own children. Learning how to handle these kinds of behaviour and involvement in parent support groups were valued. Ruth's mother talks of how the teachers 'taught us how to help Ruth'. Both William and Richard's mothers talk of how much they learned from the support groups about child management and creating a calm home environment. Student social workers were involved in co-working the support groups, participating in a complementary health programme and teaching parents how to play with each other and with their children. Providing the setting in which parents can learn new skills and adapt existing ones, and the ability to teach these skills, is a core part of these parents' positive experiences.

3 Collaborating to link home and school

'Something that was really helpful was being able to ask questions and find out what was going on at school.'

The ability of the school-based services to work together with the children's home lives is key to the way in which this work was experienced positively by the children and families. Family work takes place alongside educational and behavioural support for children and, through the student unit, there is a social work presence in the school.

The social work students are instrumental in creating a strong link between home and school. They sustained a service that is clearly valued by parents. William's mother valued having somebody you can talk to who has seen your child and is based in the school. The parents felt confidence in the social work students because the students knew their children. Ruth's mother talks of how much more helpful it is to have this personal contact from someone who is based in the school and knows your child. 'You can find out much more about your child than reading what is written in books or on bits of paper.'

4 Meeting the needs and wishes of the parents

'I suffer from depression and they lifted me out of that and made me see that I can get on without having to be depressed all the time.'

Although the central focus of everybody's concerns is the child, the student social workers demonstrate their concern for the needs and wishes of the parents, too. When these are addressed it transforms the parents' ability to cope with the stress. The groups specifically for parents are valued as an opportunity for sharing and, most of all, 'realising you are not on your own'. This 'all in the same boat' effect is commonly associated with groupwork (Doel, 2006). The support offered to them in their own homes was also identified as valuable, as time for themselves, with someone who will listen. The social work students offered a helpful external perspective for the parents. Richard's mother talks of how useful it was to have someone who was 'outside the family, so it was easier for them to see what was going on'. Alan's mother talked of being put in touch 'with organisations which would help *me*'.

5 Responding early

'I feel when the social services do get brought in, it is usually at the very last minute.'

Alan's grandmother talks of the reality of social services intervention being at times of crisis and about 'a lot of children out there suffering'. Her observations speak powerfully about the wish for early intervention and preventive work, a recurring theme in many of the stories in this book. She also talks about the benefit of access for all children to therapeutic work, such as those offered by the school, in order to get the right help at the right time.

6 Developing community resources to reduce social isolation

'I think it would be helpful for me and my family to have services in the community for children with special needs.'

All of the parents were socially isolated because of the problems they were experiencing with their children. This ranged from being unable to engage in ordinary activities like social outings, going for walks, being able to go out on your own, doing the supermarket shopping, to overt hostility from others because of the threats, perceived and real, that their children posed to others. Richard's mother experienced long periods of depression and she highlights the discrimination faced by her son, even as a baby.

The lack of ordinary community resources – no clubs, cubs or play schemes that could understand and cope with the children – was a common theme for parents. As a consequence, the children were socially impoverished as much as their parents. Richard's mother says with passion, 'I feel we should actually recognise them as normal human beings and give them the same courtesies that we give to other children and other people in the community, because they deserve it just as much as anybody else.'

To what extent is the social work role and task concerned with developing community resources? Some might suggest that this is the work of others, such as community development and youth workers, but social work has a strong historical tradition of community action, not just working with the community, but helping to mobilise it to create or lobby for resources.

7 Expecting positive change

'The school has done a lot with him and slowly but surely a year has gone by.'

We have learned that the school has a 'can do' ethos. Over time and with patience, this nurtures children towards positive change. Parents talked of the transformation that this had produced for the lives of their children and, indeed, their own, '100 per cent improvement'. Ruth's and Richard's mothers spoke of a gradual improvement, one that took time. All of this requires the belief that positive change is possible, and social workers have a large part to play in assisting these feelings of self-belief. Richard's mother talked of her depression and how the student social workers helped to lift her out of it. We do not know the details of how they did this, but an expectation of positive change is likely to have been central to this improvement.

It is always a difficult balance between accepting the pain and sadness of people as we find them, and offering the prospect of a more positive future. Usually, people want to be heard first before they can attend to the possibility of change. However, the worker's belief that positive change is both possible and to be expected can have a powerful impact on people's own self-belief. When this message is coming not just from the social worker but also from the school where they are based, this is a doubly powerful message.

8 Challenging past experiences of social work

'I had student social workers to support me as well and they certainly gave me a new outlook on social workers.'

The testimonies of the parents and the views of the children, expressed through their drawings, demonstrate the positive contribution that student social workers made to their lives. Richard's mother talked of how she 'could not have managed' without the support. Helen's research project indicates that they made a difference. Significantly, parents talked of the students overturning their negative opinions of social workers, to the extent that they would recommend their involvement to other parents.

This is an important message for all of us. Whether we believe that the kind of positive practices that have been presented in this book are regular or rare, or somewhere in between, these parents show us that it is possible to reverse previous bad experiences of social workers, and to challenge poor images of social work. Moreover, it was students who were able to trigger these new views of social work. They have been able to work positively with the parents and children, whilst making use of good practice learning and supervision.

9 Promoting evidence-informed practice

Incidents of violence fell overall, particularly those directed towards staff.

This chapter presents the work of a practice teacher who is modelling evidence-informed practice. She shows how she has evaluated the work of the school and of the student social workers by interviewing service users, seeking their views and information about their experiences in order improve the quality of the service. This was followed up with a small quantitative research study, which indicated the efficacy of the approach. She is developing herself as a practitioner researcher, which is an important element in maintaining and developing good social work practice.

In conclusion, it is evident that the parents and grandparents were very concerned for these children and told these stories from the child's perspective. This concern sits alongside descriptions of the exhaustion and agony of living with an emotionally and behaviourally disturbed child. A fundamentally important message is to resist blaming parents for the behaviour of their children but to seek with them an understanding and an empathy with the child, and to work together on the journey towards change.

The last words should belong to Helen who, in addition to offering us the results of her work, was interviewed to help us with the writing of this chapter. She remarked: 'Even where there are grave concerns, there are ways of moving forward, by working alongside families to address their needs in a timely way. Often they are seen as bad parents, their children labelled and they have lost all hope in professionals. Parents can become part of that group, condemned and labelled. Intense support makes parents feel safe and comfortable in their own zone and makes them want to stay there. The biggest lesson our service users have taught us is how socially isolated they are. That is why making sound links with the community is so important.'

Summary of learning points from the families' stories

1 Being knowledgeable
2 Teaching skills
3 Collaborating to link home and school
4 Meeting needs and responding to wishes of parents
5 Responding early
6 Developing community resources to reduce social isolation
7 Expecting positive change
8 Challenging past experiences of social work
9 Promoting evidence-informed practice

11 Learning from Positive Experiences: key themes

'Then two years ago my social worker changed ... my relationship has changed beyond belief'

Is it possible or desirable to attempt practice guidance on the basis of the stories told in this book? Certainly, others have advocated for the development of readily available, accessible and professionally sanctioned practice guidelines that can be used by practitioners working with different groups and settings (Lymbery and Butler, 2004; Rosen and Proctor, 2003). Cree and Davis (2007) helpfully conclude their collection of 'voices from the inside' of social work with some overall themes to develop good practice.

In Chapter 1 we criticised lists of 'oughts' that exhort social workers to do this and not do that, or the collections of bullet-points which, once ticked off, can seem to excuse the ticker from any further thought or action. So, what follows is presented as connecting themes arising from the stories recounted in this book, *not* a list of must do's. Of course, these themes do provide pointers to good practice but, as we hope has become evident, they are complex, inter-related and do not lend themselves readily to a thin list of injunctions.

As we noted in the introductory chapter, the stories told here have not been selected in a systematic fashion, so we must be open to the possibility of other factors playing an important part in positive experiences for other people. For instance, although only John (Chapter 8) identified faith or spirituality as important, there is evidence that this can be significant for some service users (Jenkins, 2004). However, we can be reasonably confident that a practitioner who is sensitive to the nine themes discussed below would become alert to a person's spirituality and respond in ways that were experienced positively.

Finally, what differences might there be between creating a positive experience of social work when the person is a willing partner in the relationship and when they are an involuntary participant? First, we should remember that the difference between 'voluntary' and 'involuntary' is seldom clearcut. Humerah frequently moved between the two, but her positive experience depended not on the social worker changing fundamental practices from one situation to the other, but on a practice that was able to accommodate the two. The families in Chapter 10 were suspicious at first, with stereotypes of social workers as people who took children away from families. Julia initially resented the requirement for social work intervention in her search for her birth mother. It is common for many of the people who experience social work to be, at best, ambivalent about it. We suspect that the nine themes below are as relevant to work with people who would rather not shake hands with social work as to those who embrace it.

1 Information and privacy

Many people noted their desire that information about them should be gathered and used carefully. Their positive experience of social work was built on a sense that the social worker was using information responsibly. It was recognised that mistakes are made, especially around the sharing of information, but an attention to the sensitive nature of personal knowledge is appreciated. The significance of confidentiality has been noted in other studies (Bland et al., 2006).

We found that people were also aware of the limitations to confidentiality. The self-advocates were explicit about these limits, but *they wanted social workers who would talk to them first about what information they felt they needed to share and with whom* (p. 95). For John (Chapter 8), the sharing of information between the professionals involved in his care was very productive and he views this as good practice: 'they all seemed to know what the plan was for me and to know how I wanted things to be done'. If we need any convincing about the significance of the way in which information is documented, we can find this in Richardson's (2003) personal account of the impact and effect which the collation and sharing of information can have on a family during the course of a child protection investigation. Positive experience of practice is as much dependent on *how* the process of information sharing is conducted as much as *what* that information is and on an understanding of the difference between confidentiality and privacy (Collingridge et al., 2001).

Information is a two-way process. How much information might people want or need about the organisations whose services they use? For example, is it relevant to know about the nature and composition of multi-disciplinary teams (Meddings and Perkins, 1999)? Humerah found it somewhat liberating when her growing trust in the social worker meant that she no longer felt she had to get to grips with the details of the agency's budgets and internal workings. Similarly, we can travel on a train successfully without knowing the signalling arrangements, but we do want to have confidence that there is someone who *does* know and is acting on this knowledge. The parents were very clear about the need for the worker or student to have clinical knowledge, but such that they could translate professional language into accessible information (Learning from Families, p. 112). The worker's knowledge of community resources was significant for Mrs Corbett, as was the worker's increasing knowledge of her husband which meant that *'she could anticipate if he was getting over-anxious'* (p. 33). The families in Chapter 10 wanted social workers to be knowledgeable about sources of help and support in the community and were reassured that the social worker knew their children in the context of their school.

2 Power and control

Control is a recurring theme through many, perhaps all, of the stories. It is a core issue in professional practice and strongly linked to questions of power and participation. Mrs Corbett's remark that *'at one point the social worker took over marvellously, but it's OK because I feel in charge'* challenges us to investigate the paradoxes within this notion of control, because what she says seems, on the surface, to be self-contradictory. It is Humerah's story that most starkly demonstrates the complexities, giving powerful insights into how control can be experienced across an enormous span, calibrated expertly by the service user herself. What is clear is that control is not something that is or can be 'given' or 'given over'; nor is control a crude matter of who gets their way. Indeed, for John it is control of an internal mental state that is at issue. Through the social work he regained control over his body, feeling once more the 'expert over my body'. This was liberating and enabled him to envisage a future for himself.

Humerah's story led us to consider control not as something finite and static, but in terms of a continuum, with a pointer that is capable of being swung in one direction towards service user in total control and back in the other towards no control at all. The significant question is not necessarily *where does the arrow point?* but *whose hands are on it?* In other words, how are the decisions about the degree of control made? Humerah's experience teaches us that both the service user and the social worker must share this responsibility.

The education and access to resources which comes with the social worker's turf adds power to the work and it would be irresponsible for the worker to pretend otherwise. The social worker has an added responsibility to explore the whole question of control and how it is to be determined and used, so that it is at the centre of the work. This might require many to re-examine their notion of 'professionalism' (Maidment, 2006).

Acceptable ways of negotiating, sharing and holding control are likely to vary from person to person and time to time. So, the context influences this question of control and how it is shared. Leone's story is an example of how a social worker took initial total control at the point where an emergency placement was needed. However, she then shifted to share control with Leone in relation to the suitability of the placement. There can be no single template for what is often called 'empowering practice'. There are guiding principles, such as the ones outlined in this chapter, but their relative significance will differ between persons and situations. What social workers must be able to do is to take the time to listen to the people with whom they work, and to act on what they learn from this experience, ensuring that issues of control are central, open and above board, even when control is not being exercised fully by the service user.

These stories have focused on power and control at the interpersonal level and there are increasing expectations that people should be able to lead and direct their own care and support (Swift, 2002). However, we should also consider how these issues of power and control play at a service level, for instance in a vision of social care based on social models of support and a rights-based approach (Beresford and Branfield, 2004). So, it is not just a question of creating choices within a service, but also *between* them and, increasingly, including providers of services who are, themselves, service users.

3 Acceptance and difference

Many people are in situations where they are already feeling judged and blamed by the time they encounter social work. Worst of all, they may be doing this blaming themselves and 'needing social work' only worsens this. Parents whose children's behaviour is causing concern receive the implicit and explicit message that it is their parenting that causes the poor behaviour and, therefore, that they are to blame (Chapter 10, Learning from Families). Whatever circumstances have led people to seek social work help or to have social work intervention forced upon them, they are likely to indicate some difference from social norms and, whilst some people can embrace this difference, most are likely to be distressed by the gap between the ideal sense of self and the reality.

Social workers have a significant part to play in fostering a sense of acceptance of the person, even when it is not an acceptance of the behaviour. Understanding why people might find themselves in their current circumstances and not rushing to judgement is something to be valued. It helps people who have made harsh self-judgements to begin to feel more comfortable with themselves. Acceptance does not mean

lack of challenge or change. For example, parents can be given opportunities to consider different approaches with their children without
being blamed for the current difficulties. Mandy was able to see
how she was treating her son as an emotional partner and, though
understandable, that this was not acceptable. It was a non-blaming
insight (p. 29).

Service users' current stories may have been largely scripted by other
people such as family, friends and other professionals. Julia's script was
written by the sense of precariousness as an adopted child, needing to
be well behaved in order to secure her future. In these circumstances,
acceptance does not mean adherence to these scripts; indeed, the
worker can help people to challenge the way in which their story has
been constructed. The importance of this kind of critique, often linking
wider social issues with people's individual stories, is key to social
work's holistic approach. However, there is a difference between
helping someone to reconstruct their own story and imposing yet
another professional's interpretation of their situation (Darling et al.,
2002). John 're-invented' himself, rejecting the life scripts that had
been written by others, where he 'seemed always to be struggling with
shaking off the belief that people thought I was different, odd or not
quite hitting the mark'.

Once a person feels accepted for who they are, put at ease and not
clumped into some stereotypical group, the worker might bring some
difference into the situation. This difference might lie in biography, for
instance that the worker is black and the service user is white, or in
their professional experience which is used to give the service user confidence to reconstruct their situation from a different perspective and
challenge other people's tellings of their own story – a self-acceptance
based on self-knowledge, as demonstrated by Leone's story. 'Matching'
service users and workers could lose the potential for creative differences and none of the service users specifically related their positive
experience to the fact that their worker was 'like' them. Humerah noted
the fact that her worker was Asian as a bonus, but also reflected that,
though the outside world would see them as very similar, in fact they
had very different South Asian backgrounds. Matching for similarity
might be more significant in mentoring relationships; for example,
young people at risk in the community particularly valued mentors
who shared and were willing to discuss similar backgrounds and
experiences (Philip et al., 2004). John notes a desire to mentor young
people who are grappling with mental distress. He views his story
and his recovery as being capable of bringing hope to others in similar
circumstances.

As well as acceptance of the individual, social work has a mission to
campaign for wider, social acceptance with and for social groups that

are often excluded from the mainstream. Some of these groups advocate well for themselves, others need all the support they can get. Many of the self-advocates in Chapter 9 echoed this view of the social work task. Barry said that he thinks the *'social worker's main job is to help service users to socialise and to get accepted into the community'* (p. 97). Community resources are critical to transform this desire for inclusiveness into a reality. Social workers need to give active support to community initiatives that promote social acceptance, such as those described by the self-advocates and the families in Chapters 9 and 10 and the example of 'De Caf', a dementia cafe where people with dementia and their carers can spend an enjoyable time, share problems and obtain information and support in an inclusive environment (Redwood et al., 2005).

4 Boundaries and risk

Mandy valued the space that the social worker gave to her to speak about herself. This developed her insight into her situation (p. 28). Although the worker provided a model as a supportive and critical adult, she was careful not to become a substitute partner for Mandy; so, alongside a feeling of closeness, the dialogue between Mandy and the worker was conducted within clear boundaries.

The sense of the worker as a person, someone to get to know rather than 'a suit' seems crucial to positive practice. The student social worker who went on long muddy walks with John (p. 79) helped him talk in a way that a face-to-face session in the counselling room might not. Service users prefer a sense of equality in the relationship, flexibility and going the extra distance (Ribner and Knei-Paz, 2002). Perhaps this is associated with the ability to self-disclose, albeit within careful limits. Mrs Corbett noted that the two social workers she felt positive about *had experienced unhappiness themselves*; we know, then, that they self-disclosed, though not to the extent that Mrs Corbett felt burdened or embarrassed. We do not know whether Mrs Corbett is aware *what* the unhappiness was, or just that the workers experienced it, and we do not need to know. Leone learned that her worker had personal experience of discrimination and this helped Leone to trust her to explore her own growing experiences of discrimination in the work place. We should recognise, too, that social workers can have dual relationships, for example as a practitioner and someone who uses mental health services (Reamer, 2003). There are not, of course, two self-contained groups of people, those who provide services and those who receive them. In the words of one homeless youngster interviewed by another homeless youngster, what they wanted from a social worker was 'someone who treats you as an ordinary human being' (De Winter and Noom, 2003).

John talks of feeling relieved when he detected that he 'had a chance of being seen as normal'.

Self-disclosure provides a measure of reciprocity in the relationship. The worker does not need to be experiencing the same feelings as the service user, but the act of revealing something is experienced as reciprocal. It is the power of reciprocal relationships that makes groupwork such an attractive form of practice. Indeed, for Maidment (2006), notions of reciprocity shade into compassion and even love, thus challenging conventional teaching about social worker – client relationships.

Mrs Corbett appreciates her worker's frankness: *she would say "Oh, this is a load of rubbish!" when something just wasn't right'* (p. 38). The boundary between frankness that inspires a feeling of 'in it together but we'll get the better of it' and dismay that suggests 'this is beyond me and I'm not responsible' is close, and one which these social workers judged well. It is another form of self-disclosure, of the kind of person the worker is.

If players went on to a football pitch without any knowledge of the rules we might expect people to get hurt. There are similar risks, social and emotional rather than physical, when there is a failure to discuss the 'rules of play' for social work. The need to establish groundrules is commonly accepted in groupwork practice (Doel 2006), yet seems far from routine in one-to-one work. When it happens, as with Humerah and her social worker, it contributes to the positive experience (p. 17).

One of the most difficult boundaries to work with is touch. Anxieties about the use of touch in work with children are not new (Ward, 1990), but Leone reminds us how important it can be with the right person at the right time: *'Nora made me laugh and she was very "mumsie". By that I mean she was very tactile. I was not used to being cuddled and it was Nora who taught me how to give and receive cuddles. Avril would give me a gentle pat but for cuddles it was Nora'* (p. 53). Although the literature on risk tends to focus on the balance between individuals' rights and notions of social protection, it is perhaps in the everyday balance of risks around self-disclosures, touch and the like, that the accumulation of good practice is to be found. It is significant that a study of ethics complaints against social workers found that half of these were related to violations of a professional boundary (Strom-Gottfried, 1999).

Bound up with risk-taking is trust. Only when there is a sense of trust can the kinds of risk that we have described be taken with confidence. The right balance enables a shift from, for example, a child protection to a child welfare mindset (Spratt and Callan, 2004). When mistakes are made, as they will be, it is the foundation of trust that helps the work to continue. It is reasonable to assume that trust is dependent, amongst other things, on establishing and respecting agreed boundaries.

Maybe those who handle boundaries best are those who can be honest with themselves about a degree of deception that is necessary to maintain those boundaries, be they in professional or personal lives. Although deception is usually considered a violation of trust, it is typically used in negotiating identity, maintaining self-esteem, protecting privacy, and redressing imbalances in power (Kagle, 1998). Is some kind of deception necessary to manage the boundaries in professional relationships and are some kinds of deception more 'honest' than others? By its very nature, deception is not disclosed, so it is difficult to know how self-aware (honest) deception might have had a part to play in contributing to the positive experiences in this book. Certainly, a worker who pretends that the organisation's systems always operate with complete fairness and competence is practising *dishonest* self-deception and is likely to lose the service user's confidence. The same is true of workers who dissociate themselves entirely from their agency as though they are not at all complicit with its activities.

5 Practical support and emotional intelligence

The seminal work on clients' views of social work, *The Client Speaks* (Mayer and Timms, 1970) highlighted the significance of practical and financial help and, sadly, the gap between this reality and the professionals' perceptions.

More recently, Bland et al's (2006) consultations with service users highlighted practical support as a key factor. Several stories in this book confirm the importance of practical support and, happily, the positive response of the workers. For Mandy (p. 27) this amounted to learning specific techniques to improve the situation, whilst for many of the self-advocates (p. 96) it was the workers' willingness to get to know them by joining in activities. Nina recounts how *the student social worker did all the paperwork, the housing claim, income benefit, disability allowance, the lot* (p. 44). This was not experienced as taking over, but as providing urgent and immediate assistance. The families in Chapter 10 suggested that social workers should address the absence of practical support and develop new services that met the need of parents and children for practical support.

Balancing the willingness to respond with immediate action, is the ability to demonstrate emotional intelligence (Goleman, 1996). All of the workers in these stories demonstrate empathy and an ability to communicate this. They are emotionally attuned to the people they are working with. One indication of this is the ability not just to recognise but to anticipate feelings. This was important for Mrs Corbett, perhaps because it made her feel she had company in looking after her husband before he died (p. 36). Julia's emotions overwhelmed her at times, and her social worker helped her to explore anticipated emotions as a rehearsal for the events that would change her greatly (p. 71).

The combination of practical support and emotional intelligence reflects the holistic basis of social work. In responding to the whole person in their world, perhaps the service user sees the social worker as a whole person, too. We will return to the notion of holistic practice in Section 9.

6 Rhythm and continuity

Each encounter between two or more people develops its own rhythm and social work encounters are no different. What seems important is the ability to respond to and create the rhythms of different encounters. This is especially notable in Humerah's story, where fluctuations in the state of her mental health required a social work response that was highly adaptive and that could recognise patterns in the rhythms (p. 16). It required the social worker to take a quite opposite tack depending on the trough or peak of Humerah's life.

First impressions are significant and accessibility is consistently mentioned as important to people using social work services, too often in complaint of their absence: 'they only come when I'm in trouble, not when I ask them ... my mum phones them, they tell my mum they'll be there but they don't come' (Crickmay, 2005). Accessibility, or lack of it, sets the tone for our relationship with a service, whatever it is. Do we speak to an informed person immediately or do we have to pursue a long trail of menus on the phone to end up listening to a pre-recorded message? Do we have to wait in all day because the service will not give us a precise time for delivery? Is the experience of being a client of the agency respectful or humiliating (Ronning, 2005)? John's story emphasises the distress caused by lengthy referral processes.

For most people a speedy response is appreciated. '*It was really important to have someone quick*', notes Mandy (p. 26). Others remark on the benefit of early intervention before situations deteriorate, '*getting the right help at the right time*', as one of the families remarks (p. 113). Once the initial contact has been made, it is the regularity of contact that helps to establish a rhythm. As Nina notes, '*even when there wasn't any particular news she would just give a quick call to let me know she was still on the case*' (p. 46). Regular contact gives the social worker a kind of presence even when they are not there; if things are difficult people can hang on to their troubles until the next contact because they know they can rely on it happening. It is this reliability that begins to develop a sense of rhythm, a continuity that is experienced as positive.

John talks of how the continuing and reliable support of his social worker, even when he moved to London, gave him a sense of safety. He became skilled in knowing when to call on his social worker and expresses some pride in his need for reduced contact as his recovery proceeds.

Humerah found her rhythm with one social worker, but she did not experience it with others. Mrs Corbett was more fortunate and she experienced a continuity of *service* so that when one social worker left, her successor maintained a similar pace and pattern. *Mrs Corbett seems to have benefited from a positive service, not just from positive social workers* (p. 40). We will consider in Chapter 12 how positive practice can build into a positive service.

The service users in this book recognised that social workers have lives and careers and that these will sometimes take them on to other things. However, some, such as David, were clear about the etiquette of moving on and that positive experiences of social work depended on a sense of continuity in the *service* if not the person (p. 100). Endings and transitions have their own rhythms, too. The workers who were special in Leone's life *went the extra mile* and the worker from her second placement continued contact in the third (p. 58, 59). We saw in Chapter 1 how other accounts of children in care make it clear that they would like support in keeping in touch with friends they have made before care, and that they do not wish to see good relationships with professionals squandered by automatically terminating them when either the worker or the child moves on (Voice for the Child in Care, 2004).

One of the authors regularly continued to work with service users when they moved out of the 'patch' area, at least until they were settled in the new location and there had been opportunity for joint work with the new worker. An American study found that caregiver reports of having less than two child welfare workers were associated with higher perceived quality of relationships with child welfare workers (Chapman et al., 2003) and another study reported that continuity was one of six key aspects of quality in the life of older people being maintained at home (Francis and Netten, 2004). The evidence is clear that continuity is critical; where possible a more imaginative approach to continuity of person is needed to prevent people worrying 'how long am I going to see you before you change into someone else?' (John, p. 78).

7 Planning and networking

A study of a multi-disciplinary team found that the other professions in the team had a clear understanding of the social work contribution and that this was valued positively: 'I think what is valuable is [social work] having a broader, all encompassing view of the community and the people and what's out there. A much wider picture than some of the other disciplines' (Herod and Lymbery, 2002: 21). The stories in this book also suggest that service users and carers appreciate the wider view of the community that social workers can bring. This is not just a question of putting people in touch with community resources, such as

Mr Corbett and the group for people with sight and hearing problems, but also creating choices and helping with decisions. This active planning builds bridges between service users and other professionals, too. The early intervention service in Chapter 9 deliberately seeks to locate its activities with service users in ordinary, age-appropriate settings, emphasising the significance of work and continuing education to the recovery of mental health. John talks of learning to 'use the community as a resource rather than staying within mental health services excusively'.

The social worker was a conduit between Julia and her birth family, the stage manager for the first contact between them (p. 72); and for the families in Chapter 10 the social workers were the main link between home and school. Sometimes it is the service user's own networks that the social worker will help to maintain, especially when these 'networks are the family I did not have' (Leone, p. 54).

Planning is linked to the rhythms we mentioned in the preceding section. It is the regularity of Nina's student social worker that enables their plans to be faithfully and persistently carried through. Nina develops a confidence that plans will be developed participatively and that the student will be reliable in following through. Nor do the small details go un-noticed: *'even in really bad rain she'd come here to do the forms'* (p. 42). The outcome of the student's networking with the Housing Department and her business-like persistence is clear to Nina: *'I wouldn't have this property if not for her'* (p. 42). And she has a message for the service: *'she should be the manager, she should be the one telling people what to do'* (p. 43).

Planning for a service and not just an individual encounter may well entail seeking out the views of people who are not currently service users, but who are potentially so. This kind of planning goes further than the individual plans that characterise most of the stories in the book.

8 Belief and purposive relationships

Perhaps the most encouraging message that comes from these stories is the difference that a single worker can make: *'Then, two years ago, my social worker changed and my social work relationship has changed beyond belief'* (p. 10). Without wishing to put too much responsibility on the shoulders of one person, we learn from Humerah that even the weight of 18 years' negative experiences can be transformed speedily by just one person.

Also of significance is the re-emergence of the relationship, not as an end in itself, but as an important vehicle for the work. At the heart of the relationship is the worker's belief in the possibility of change and an expressed belief in the service user. Leone's extraordinary story is testimony to how the belief in someone can give them the strength to succeed (p. 60). The way in which this belief is expressed will vary, so that for Nina it was the social work student's persistence; for the families it was the workers' expectations of positive change that gave them self-belief.

Strengths-based practice in social work has a strong theoretical foundation, but accounts of how individuals who receive these services view their experiences are patchy (Brun and Rapp, 2001). The stories in this book give us a direct window onto what strengths-based theory can mean in practice and how this cultivates resilience (Greene, 2002). Mrs Corbett's resilience after her husband died was boosted by her workers' belief in her, as was Leone's.

9 Contexts

There are many kinds of context to consider. Given that this book is based on personal stories, it is understandable that the significance of the individual service user's context comes to the fore. For example, Mrs Corbett valued the curiosity that her workers showed about her and her husband's lives as a whole: *it is important to Mrs Corbett that the workers appreciate her and her husband as people who are more than the sum of their needs and disabilities; people with a history as well as a present* (p. 38).

Taking the trouble, and the risk, to go beyond the 'script' is experienced positively. *Nina appreciates the fact that the student takes time to find out about her as a whole person, not just 'someone with a literacy problem' or 'someone with accommodation needs'. The student spends time with Nina's husband, too, and no doubt pays attention to the children. This reflects the fact that Nina is not an isolated individual but a person in a wider context of family, friends and community* (p. 47). Although it is the children who are the central focus of concern in the family stories, the parents value the fact that the social workers and students considered their needs too (p. 113).

However, there are other contexts which contribute to these positive experiences, notably the community. The self-advocates note the capacity of social workers to open doors to the community (p. 97), the families think social work has an important role in developing and supporting inclusive community resources to help reduce social isolation (p. 114).

Social workers have a central role in negotiating with the wider professional community, too. Whether it is interpreting other professions' jargon, helping colleagues to see the situation from the service user's perspective or accessing resources controlled by other professional groups, social workers are valued for their active advocacy. *'The social worker battled for us,'* says Mrs Corbett (p. 33).

Social workers are members of their own professional community, one which subscribes to an ethical code of practice (GSCC, 2002) and is built on a growing body of evidence and knowledge. This 'community of practice' (Wenger, 1998) does not perhaps have as strong an influence as the immediate agency context (see Chapter 12), but it does expect workers to contribute to practice development. This is especially evident in the worker with the families (p. 115).

For the large part social workers are not independent clinicians in the UK. They work primarily for agencies, largely in the statutory sector, but increasingly in voluntary, independent and private settings. Though largely unseen by service users and carers, the context of this work setting has an enormous impact (Marsh and Triseliotis, 1996). People will differ in the extent that they want to know the details of this context and this will probably relate to how satisfied they feel with the service. It is interesting that Humerah came to the conclusion that *it was the worker's job to know what was and was not possible with her agency* (p. 22) only when she had confidence in her social worker. At that point she did not feel the need to know how policies were being intepreted in practice, and how problems in the field were transmitted to the policy level (Ahmad, 2003). However, the mechanisms by which this information becomes policy is of great significance to the service and, with eligibility criteria, might define or exclude someone from that service.

There are wider contexts still, such as the social policy, legal and political contexts. Sometimes these will make their presence felt directly and visibly, such as the adoption laws for Julia (p. 71); at other times their influence may be critical, yet pass unrecognised. In the Canadian context, increasing poverty among families with children, and the effects of the introduction of a legalistic, investigative agenda for child protection services has been associated with negative experiences of social work (Palmer et al., 2006).

This all begs the question as to the extent to which social work practice should be politically oriented (Shamai and Boehm, 2001) and, if so, how this can best be expressed. It is perhaps the linking of individual people's experiences to social welfare policy that marks social work's distinctiveness; its unique contribution being its broad contextualised approach to human needs (Barnes and Hugman, 2002; Stuart, 1999). We can only extrapolate the way in which these other contexts are experienced by service users and carers because they are usually implicit in their stories. How evident is a commitment to social justice through the individual experiences related in this book? It is ironic that Leone experienced care as 'a cocoon' which therefore did not prepare her for adult encounters with racism and discrimination (p. 51).

We discussed trust in the context of the relationship between worker and service user, but it is also a broader issue at other levels, between workers and agencies, agencies and government. It is a contentious matter as to how and whether trust can be re-discovered at these levels (Smith, 2001). Just as service users need to experience practitioners' belief in them, so practitioners also need to experience the trust of government and agencies, if they are to develop confident practice.

Summary of key themes

1 **Information and privacy:** sensitivity about collecting information and using it; discussion about confidentiality and its limits; having workers who are knowledgeable and can communicate well

2 **Power and control:** service users and professionals must share responsibility for decisions about control; there is no single template for empowerment

3 **Acceptance and difference:** not rushing to judgement, but also making appropriate challenges or 'non-blaming insights'; campaigning alongside service users for wider social acceptance of difference

4 **Boundaries and risk:** flexibility, reciprocity and equality in relationships whilst knowing the limits; someone who treats you as an ordinary human being; discussing 'the rules'; developing trust and taking risks

5 **Practical support and emotional intelligence:** being active with regular practical support; joining in activities; recognising and anticipating feelings; holistic approaches which combine practical and emotional support

6 **Rhythm and continuity:** responding to and creating different rhythms according to the encounter; accessibility, early interventions and speedy responses; regularity and reliability; continuity of service from one practitioner to another

7 **Planning and networking:** having a wide view of people's lives and opportunities; creating choices and helping with decisions; making links with the wider community; building networks and developing plans participatively

8 **Belief and purposive relationships:** believing in people, in the possibility of change and that you and they can make a difference; cultivating resilience

9 **Contexts:** curiosity about the person as a whole, their lives and their community; negotiating with other professions; capacity to work the agency to the service users' advantage; understanding of social policy and legislation and the political context

12 From Positive Practices to a Positive Service

Nina muses that it is a matter of luck as to who [which social worker] you get

We acknowledged in the introduction to this book that it is not possible to estimate the extent of positive experiences of social work. We suspect that they are more common than the fascination with pathological social work suggests. Whatever the actual prevalence, it is fortunate that we can learn immensely from just *one* positive experience. If we are to construct the idea of social work through an understanding of what happens when people experience it, we should ensure that this construct is informed by lessons drawn from positive experience. In this way we are more likely to develop practices that are more effective in meeting people's aspirations. Although we do not as yet have a clear evidence base, it seems reasonable to assume that listening to these positive experiences can help move away from notions of 'clienthood' (Hall, 2003) towards a more equal partnership, in which social work is constructed by people – service user, practitioner, manager or policy-maker – on more equal terms.

The alternative to this approach is to continue to base practice development either on highly unusual instances of catastrophic social work, or on the general background hum of existing practice, uncodified and unseen.

The construction of social work is, of course, more than the sum of these encounters. We must recognise that in addition to the immediate contextual factors in any particular encounter between practitioner and service user there is a wider context of team, agency, profession, social policy, law, regulation and public expectations. All of these shape and shade the experience of social work. However, what is striking about the stories in this book, especially Humerah's, is the way in which an individual worker changed an individual service user's total experience. Neither the team nor the agency, nor the profession, social policy, law, regulatory framework, nor public expectations changed when one social worker took the place of another. All that changed was the social worker. Can it be, then, that there has been a tendency to over-emphasise the wider contextual factors and to under-estimate the significance of the individual worker? The most influential voices are those of the academics and the policy makers and it is possible that their fascinations are more with the wider contextual issues than the daily detail of practice, so that the latter has been relegated to the shade. This is all rather tentative, but it does suggest an urgent need to give stronger voice to those who experience social work directly – service users, carers and practitioners.

What we cannot know from these stories is the extent to which the 'nouse' of the social worker depended on the way they managed these contextual factors. In other words, although the only change for Humerah was a different social worker, perhaps this social worker had the desire and the ability to work with policy both at street level and at the formal level. Musil et al. (2004) describe two kinds of street-level policy – the one in which workers avoid the dilemmas of their work without trying to change those uncertain conditions that provoke these dilemmas, and the other in which practitioners try to negotiate the uncertain working conditions that are at the roots of their dilemmas. We suspect the latter is experienced as the more positive practice, though it may not be conceptualised as such either by the service user or the practitioner.

How can we develop a positive service, not just a positive encounter? For all the excellent work done by Humerah's social worker she could not ensure that these positive experiences would continue once she had left the agency (see the Epilogue to this chapter). How might the worker's team, supervisor and agency have learned from this good practice in ways that enabled it to endure? It is important to establish an effective feedback loop – a continuous evaluation with systematic ways of collecting and disseminating findings from these evaluations. How can an agency become aware of the dramatic turnaround in fortunes in the work with Humerah? Once aware, surely an agency must find out more about what brought about these changes and what lessons they hold for its services as a whole?

In addition to its own staff, the agency's service users are its best resource. Any evaluation of services must involve those who use them, and this is more likely to be effective if it is embedded in a systematic fashion, for example via a service user and carer forum. There are systematic models of evaluation, such as Appreciative Inquiry, which use positive methods with the intent of building and learning from positive experiences (Appreciative Inquiry, 2006).

Continuity of contact is an interesting example of the cross-currents of person, profession and organisation. There is an understanding by service users that social workers' personal circumstances change, but David, one of the self-advocates in Chapter 9, pointed to the professional etiquette of departure he would like to see as routine practice. In addition to this, organisations have a responsibility to promote continuity by endorsing a range of measures that will encourage workers to stay. Opportunities for continuing professional development, senior career grades for practitioners, valuing professional autonomy and a supportive environment are all likely to lead to job loyalty and, therefore, to continuity for the service users (Parker et al., 2006).

There are many questions which agencies and policy makers will ask themselves if they wish to consider how the kinds of practice described in these pages might be generalised to all of social work practice. Models of delivery based on a 'general social work practitioner' based in a local community and with the degree of autonomy that general medical practitioners enjoy would be a good start. Engineering a situation in which social workers spend 80 per cent of their time in direct contact with service users and 20 per cent in meetings and administration (as opposed to the other way round) would be another.

We noted in the introductory chapter that we do not know what methods the social workers have been using, and whether they were systematic or relatively ad hoc. Research into practice methodologies is sadly tiny and underfunded, but what evidence we have suggests that some practices, such as task-centred practice, are well received (Marsh and Doel, 2005). Do service users' individual characteristics, preferences and expectations make them better suited to some approaches than others (Starin, 2006) and do some practitioners adapt better than others to these different preferences? Did other service users who experienced the same social workers who feature in this book find their experience equally positive? In other words, do the factors that made these social workers generate a positive experience of practice generalise to the rest of the people they work with? We cannot know.

In this book we have explored in detail the individual social worker's capacities, as experienced by service users and carers – this is one of the 'quadrants' in the Re-imagining Social Work project (Adnan and Kane, 2004). The other three quadrants are the practice and structure of social work, the local and general culture within which it operates, and the nature and execution of policy. Whilst acknowledging their significance, we can only touch on these other three areas.

Our purpose has been to give voice to positive experiences of social work and to reflect on the learning from these stories. It has not been our purpose to explore what prevents experiences from being positive, though there is growing evidence of some of these factors, such as stress, burnout and even fear (Lloyd et al., 2002; Smith et al., 2003). We hope this book generates optimism about the possibilities for social work, and nurtures the belief that we can make a difference. However, we cannot leave without expressing concern that most of the messages emerging from these stories are not new and yet, like the broken record technique, they seem to need re-stating.

For example, National Occupational Standards for Social Work were published in 2002 (Topss, 2002) and, as part of the development of these standards, consultations were undertaken with people who use services. From this consultation a statement of expectations from individuals, families, carers, groups and communities who use services and those who care for them was developed. The statement is organised under six headings. Key themes included clarity about roles and purpose, building honest relationships, listening actively to service users, promoting their involvement in decision making, respecting ethnicity and culture and being knowledgeable about the law and resources. Reliability and respect for confidentiality, explaining its boundaries, were viewed as central to good practice, as well as having regard for service users' expertise in their own situations. This included respecting the right to take risks and the promotion of independence.

Those consulted thought that social workers should be creative, accountable to service users for their practice and seek to put the service user in touch with others, via groups and networks. Where necessary social workers should be active in lobbying for services and should be able to challenge injustices and discrimination faced by service users. They should be able to challenge poor practice in others and in their own organizations and they should put service users first. These statements have strong echoes in the contributions that service users have made to this book.

Most elements of positive practice do not even require additional resources. Yet agencies continue to obsess about their own internal organisation and devote enormous energies to a merry-go-round of restructuring which has little, if any, connection to the world of the people who use its services. Barely has one settlement been achieved than it is torn up again in the face of a further frenzied diktat from central government. All of this serves to loosen rather than strengthen the trust in individual practitioners which is necessary if the direct experience of practice is to improve.

An increasing focus on direct practice, taking full account of the clear messages from service users and carers about what they value from social workers, will enable us to move on.

Epilogue

Humerah contacted one of the authors some time after the storytelling. 'Is the book out yet?' It was not a casual enquiry but an urgent plea. Humerah's social worker had left and it was not working out well with the new one. She desperately wanted to show her chapter so that the new worker could read about how it *could* work. It was agreed that a copy of the chapter, including the commentary, would be given to the new worker and Humerah requested that it come direct from the authors and in time for an upcoming case review meeting.

There are many lessons in this epilogue, but the one we would like to highlight is the circularity of the process of story, narration and reflection, and the fine line between research and practice, writing and doing. It is clear that the telling (and, of course, imminent publication) of Humerah's story validates it in a way that goes beyond the mere experiencing of the events. At this stage we do not know the outcome of this further chapter in Humerah's story. Optimists will hope that the new social worker has the imagination to re-view Humerah, transformed by the power of this vision of what could be. Pessimists will fear that it will push the new worker into ever-deeper defensive practice, threatened by the comparison with the predecessor rather than open to the new learning. Whatever the outcome, this epilogue underlines the power of stories.

Post-epilogue

Later still, Humerah reported that it had been decided that the new social worker would be replaced with another. The attitude of this newest worker is very positive indeed, much more like the social worker who figures in her story and completely different to the one she has just replaced. Humerah is pretty certain that this latest social worker *has* read her story.

'I have to be frank, when I volunteered my story I was sceptical about what difference telling it could make. But now I am convinced.'

References

Adnan, I. and Kane, P. (2004) *Re-imagining Social Work*. Edinburgh: Scottish Executive, The Stationery Office.

Ahmad, M.M. (2003) 'Interactions between field workers and their clients and superiors in non-governmental organisations', *Indian Journal of Social Work*, 64 (4): 463–488.

Anderson, S.C. and Mandell, D.L. (1989) 'The use of self-disclosure by professional social workers', *Social Casework*, 70 (5): 259–267.

Appreciative Inquiry (2006) http://www.aipractitioner.com (accessed November 2006).

Aubrey, C. and Dahl, S. (2006) 'Moral character in social work', *British Journal of Social Work*, 36: 75–89.

Audit Commission (2003) *Services for Disabled Children: A Review of Services for Disabled Children and Their Families*. London: The Stationery Office.

Barnes, D. and Hugman, B. (2002) 'Portrait of social work', *Journal of Interprofessional Care*, 16 (3): 277–288.

Beresford, P. and Branfield, F. (2004) 'Shape up and listen', *Community Care*, 4 November, pp. 40–41.

Beresford, P. and Croft, S. (2004) 'Service users and practitioners reunited: the key component for social work reform', *British Journal of Social Work*, 34 (1): 53–68.

Beresford, P. and Turner, M. (1997) *It's Our Welfare: Report of the Citizen's Commission on the Future of Welfare*. London: National Institute for Social Work.

Bland, R., Laragy, C., Giles, R. and Scott, V. (2006) 'Asking the consumer: exploring consumers' views in the generation of social work practice standards', *Australian Social Work*, 59 (1): 35–46.

Blueprint Project (2004) *Young people as partners in the Blueprint project: what young people had to say; what did we do*. London: Voice for the Child in Care.

Brun, C. and Rapp, R.C. (2001) 'Strengths-based case management: individuals perspectives on strengths and the case manager relationship', *Social Work*, 46 (3): 278–288.

Carr, S. (2004) *Has Service User Participation Made a Difference to Social Care Services?* London: SCIE Position Paper 3.

Carter, P., Jeffs, T. and Smith, M.K. (eds) (1995) *Social Working*. Basingstoke: Macmillan.

Chapman, M.V., Gibbons, C., Barth, R.P. and McCrae, J. (2003) 'Parental views of in-home services: what predicts satisfaction with child welfare workers?', *Child Welfare*, 82(5): 571–596.

Clark, C. (2006) 'Children's voices: the views of vulnerable children on their service providers and the relevance of services they receive', *British Journal of Social Work*, 36: 21–39.

Coates, E. (2004) '"I forgot the sky!" Children's stories contained within their drawings', V. Lewis et al.(eds), *The Reality of Research with Children and Young People*. London: SAGE/Open University, pp. 5–26.

Collingridge, M., Miller, S. and Bowles, W. (2001) 'Privacy and confidentiality in social work', *Australian Social Work*, 54 (2): 3–13.

Crawford, M.J. and Kessel, S. (1999) 'Not listening to patients – the use and misuse of patient satisfaction studies', *International Journal of Social Psychiatry*, 45: 1–6.

Cree, V. (2003) *Becoming a Social Worker*. London: Routledge.

Cree, V. and Davis, A. (2007) *Inside Social Work*. London: Routledge.

Crickmay, J. (2005) 'Getting at the truth', *Young Minds*, 77: 24.

Darling, R.B., Hager, M.A., Stockdale, J.M. and Heckert, D.A. (2002) 'Divergent views of clients and professionals: a comparison of responses to a needs assessment instrument', *Journal of Social Service Research*, 28 (3): 41–64.

De Winter, M. and Noom, M. (2003) 'Someone who treats you as an ordinary human being: homeless youth examine the quality of professional care', *British Journal of Social Work*, 33 (3): 325–337.

Devore, W. and Schlesinger, E.G. (1991) *Ethnic-Sensitive Social Work Practice*, 3rd edition. New York: Merrill Publishing.

DfES (Department for Education and Skills) (2003) *Every Child Matters*. London: The Stationery Office.

Doel, M. (2006) *Using Groupwork*. London: Routledge/Community Care.

Doel, M. and Marsh, P. (1992) *Task-Centred Social Work*. Aldershot: Ashgate.

Doel, M., Sawdon, C. and Morrison, D. (2002) *Learning, Practice and Assessment: Signposting the Portfolio*. London: Jessica Kingsley.

Every Disabled Child Matters (2006) *Off the Radar: How Local Authority Plans Fail Disabled Children*. Available at www.edcm.org.uk/pdfs/edcm_offtheradar_fullreport.pdf (accessed September 2007).

Fook, J. (2002) *Social Work: Critical Theory and Practice*. London: SAGE.

Francis, J. and Netten, A. (2004) 'Raising the quality of home care: a study of services users' views', *Social Policy and Administration*, 38 (3): 290–305.

Fraser, S., Lewis, V., Ding, S., Kellett, M. and Robinson, C. (2004) *Doing Research with Children and Young People*. London: SAGE/Open University.

Gambrill, E. (2003) 'A client-focused definition of social work', *Research on Social Work Practice*, 13 (3): 310–323.

Glasgow Media Group (1994) 'The impact of the mass media on public images of mental illness: media content and audience belief', *Health Education Journal*, 53: 271–281.

Goleman, D. (1996) *Emotional Intelligence*. London: Bloomsbury.

Greene, R.R. (2002) 'Holocaust survivors: a study in resilience', *Journal of Gerontological Social Work*, 37 (1): 3–18.

Grimshaw, R. and Sinclair, R. (1997) *Planning to Care: Regulation, Procedure and Practice Under the Children Act 1989*. London: National Childrens Bureau.

GSCC (2002) *Codes of Practice for Social Care Workers and Employers*. London: General Social Care Council, www.gscc.org.uk

Hall, C. (2003) *Constructing Clienthood in Social Work and Human Services: Interaction, Identities and Practices*. London: Jessica Kingsley.

Harding, T. and Beresford, P. (1996) *The Standards We Expect: What Service Users and Carers Want from Social Workers*. London: National Institute for Social Work.

Haulotte, S.M. and Kretzschmaur, J.A. (2001) *Case Scenarios for Teaching and Learning Social Work Practice*. London: Central Council for Education and Training in Social Work.

Heriot, J.K. and Polinger, E.J.(2002) *The Use of Personal Narratives in the Helping Professions: A Teaching Casebook*. New York: Haworth.

Herod, J. and Lymbery, M. (2002) 'The social work role in multi-disciplinary teams', *Practice*, 14 (4): 17–27.

Heus, M. and Pincus, A. (1986) *The Creative Generalist: A Guide to Social Work Practice*. Barneveld, Wisconsin: Micamar.

Hingley-Jones, H. (2005) 'An exploration of the issues raised by living with a child with autistic spectrum disorder and a professional's attempt to move beyond pity and blame', *Journal of Social Work Practice*, 19 (2): 115–129.

Horwath, J. (ed.) (2001) *The Child's World: Assessing Children in Need*. London: Jessica Kingsley.

Howe, D. and Hinings, D. (1995) 'Reason and emotion in social work practice: managing relationships with difficult clients', *Journal of Social Work Practice*, 9 (1): 5–14.

Humphries, B. (2004) 'An unacceptable role for social work: implementing immigration policy', *British Journal of Social Work*, 34 (1): 93–107.

Jenkins, C. (2004) 'Playing the game', *Counselling and Psychotherapy Journal*, 15 (8): 36–37.

Johnston, P. and Hatton, S. (2003) *Conversations in Autism: From Insight to Good Practice*. Kidderminster: British Institute of Learning Disabilities.

Kadushin, G. (1996) 'Elderly hospitalized patients' perceptions of the interaction with the social worker during discharge planning', *Social Work in Health Care*, 23(1): 1–21.

Kagle, J.D. (1998) 'Are we lying to ourselves about deception?', *Social Service Review*, 72 (2): 234–250.

Kalcher, J. (2004) 'Social group work in Germany: an American import and its historical development', in C.J. Carson, A.S. Fritz, E. Lewis, J.H. Ramey and D.T. Sugiuchi (eds), *Growth and Development Through Group Work*. Binghamton, NY: Haworth.

Lancaster, P. and Broadbent, V. (2003) *Listening to Young Children*. Maidenhead: Open University Press [11 booklets; with CD ROM].

Lecroy, C.W. (2002) *The Call to Social Work: Life Stories*. London: SAGE.

Lee, C.D. and Ayon, C. (2004) 'Is the client – worker relationship associated with better outcomes in mandated child abuse cases?', *Research on Social Work Practice*, 14 (5): 351–357.

Lewis, V., Kellett, M., Robinson, C., Fraser, S. and Ding, S. (2004) *The Reality of Research with Children and Young People*. London: SAGE/Open University.

Lloyd, C., King, R. and Chenoworth, L. (2002) 'Social work stress and burnout: a review', *Journal of Mental Health*, 11 (3): June 2002, pp. 255–265.

Lymbery, M. and Butler, S. (2004) *Social Work Ideals and Practice Realities*. Basingstoke: Palgrave Macmillan.

Maidment, J. (2006) 'The quiet remedy: a dialogue on reshaping professional relationships', *Families in Society*, 87 (1): 115–121.

Malin, N. (ed.) (2000) *Professionalism, Boundaries and the Workplace*. London: Routledge.

Malone, C., Forbat, L., Robb, M. and Seden, J. (eds) (2005) *Relating Experience: Stories from Health and Social Care*. London: Routledge.

Marquis, R. and Jackson, R. (2000) 'Quality of life and quality of services relationships: experiences of people with disabilities', *Disability and Society*, 15 (3): 411–425.

Marsh, P. and Doel, M. (2005) *The Task-Centred Book*. London: Routledge/Community Care.

Marsh, P. and Triseliotis, J. (1996) *Ready to Practise? Social Workers and Probation Officers: Their Training and First Year in Work*. Aldershot: Avebury.

Mayer, J.E. and Timms, N. (1970) *The Client Speaks*. London: Routledge and Kegan Paul.

McBride, P. (1998) *The Assertive Social Worker*. Aldershot: Arena.

McGorry, P.D. (2005) 'Early intervention in psychotic disorders: beyond debate to solving problems', *British Journal of Psychiatry*, 187 (48): 108–110.

Meddings, S. and Perkins, R. (1999) 'Service user perspectives on the rehabilitation team and roles of professionals within it', *Journal of Mental Health*, 8 (1): 87–94.

Murphy, C., Killick, J. and Allan, K. (2001) *Hearing the Users' Voice: Encouraging People with Dementia to Reflect on Their Experiences of Services*. Stirling: University of Stirling, Dementia Services Development Centre.

Musil, L., Kubalčíková, K., Hubíková, O., and Nečasová, M. (2004) 'Do social workers avoid the dilemmas of work with clients?', *European Journal of Social Work*, 7 (3): 305–319.

Napier, L. and Fook, J. (eds) (2000) *Breakthroughs in Practice: Theorising Critical Moments in Social Work*. London: Whiting and Birch.

Nerdrum, P. and Lundquist, K. (1995) ' Does participation in communication skills training increase student levels of communicated empathy? A controlled outcome study', *Journal of Teaching in Social Work*, 12 (1/2): 139–157.

Okamoto, S.K. (2003) ' The function of professional boundaries in the therapeutic relationship between male practitioners and female youth clients', *Child and Adolescent Social Work Journal*, 20 (4): 303–313.

Palmer, S., Maiter, S. and Manji, S. (2006) 'Effective intervention in child protective services: learning from parents', *Children and Youth Services Review*, 28 (7): 812–824.

Parker, J., Doel, M. and Whitfield, J. (2007) 'Does practice learning assist the recruitment and retention of staff?', *Research, Policy and Planning*, 24 (3): 179–196.

Parker, J., Whitfield, J. and Doel, M. (2006) *Improving Practice Learning in Local Authorities 2: Workforce Planning, Recruitment and Retention*. London: Skills for Care, 'Capturing the Learning' series.

Philip, K., Shucksmith, J. and King, C. (2004) *Sharing a Laugh? A Qualitative Study of Mentoring Interventions with Young People*. York: Joseph Rowntree Foundation.

Pichot, T. and Dolan, Y.M. (2003) *Solution-Focused Brief Therapy*. Binghamton, NY: The Haworth Clinical Practice Press.

Pithouse, A. (1998) *Social Work: The Social Organisation of an Invisible Trade*, 2nd edition. Aldershot: Ashgate.

Reamer, F. (2003) 'Boundary issues in social work: managing dual relationships', *Social Work*, 48 (1): 121–133.

Redwood, P., Robinson, D. and Price, J. (2005) 'De Caf: a meeting place and therapeutic resource', *Journal of Dementia Care*. 13 (4): 20–22.

Rees, S. (1978) *Social Work Face to Face: Clients and Social Workers' Perceptions of the Content and Outcomes of their Meetings*. London: Edward Arnold.

Reid, W.J. and Epstein, L. (1973) *Task-Centred Casework*. New York: Columbia University.

Ribner, D.S. and Knei-Paz, C. (2002) 'Client's view of a successful help-ing relationship', *Social Work*, 47 (4): 379–387.

Richardson, M. (2003) 'A personal reflective account: the impact of the collation and sharing of information during the course of a child protection investigation', *Child and Family Social Work*, 8 (2): 123–132.

Ronning, R. (2005) 'Do the social services in the municipalities communicate lack of respect for the clients?', *Nordisk Sosialt Arbeid*, 25 (2): 111–121.

Rosen, A. and Proctor, E.K. (2003) *Developing Practice Guidelines for Social Work Intervention: Issues, Methods, and Research Agenda*. New York: Columbia University Press.

Saarnio, P. (2000) 'Does it matter who treats you?', *European Journal of Social Work*, 3 (3): 261–268.

Sainsbury, E. (1989) 'What Clients Value' unpublished paper. London: BASW Task-Centred Practice Study Day.

Shamai, M. and Boehm, A. (2001) 'Politically orientated social work intervention', *International Social Work*, 44 (3): 343–360.

Sheppard, M. (2006) *Social Work and Social Exclusion: The Idea of Practice*. Aldershot: Ashgate.

Smith, C. (2001) 'Trust and confidence: possibilities for social work in "high modernity"', *British Journal of Social Work*, 31 (2): 287–305.

Smith, M. (2003) 'Social workers praised by service users! What the Climbié Report doesn't say', *Practice*, 15 (3): 7–16.

Smith, M., McMahon, L. and Nursten, J. (2003) 'Social workers' expe-riences of fear', *British Journal of Social Work*, 33 (5): 659–671.

Solas, J. (1995) 'Recovering and reconstructing the client's story in social work', *Australian Social Work*, 48 (3):33–36.

Spratt, T. and Callan, J. (2004) 'Parents' views on social work interven-tions in child welfare cases', *British Journal of Social Work*, 34 (2): 199–224.

Stanley, N. (1999) 'User-practitioner transactions in the new culture of community care', *British Journal of Social Work*, 29 (3): 417–435.

Starin, A. (2006) 'Clients' role choices: unexplored factors in interven-tion decisions', *Clinical Social Work Journal*, 34 (1): 101–119.

Strom-Gottfried, K. (1999) 'Professional boundaries: an analysis of vio-lations by social workers', *Families in Society*, 80 (5): 439–449.

Stuart, P.H. (1999) 'Linking clients and policy: social work's distinctive contribution', *Social Work*, 44 (4): 335–347.

Swain, P.A. (2006) 'A camel's nose under the tent? Some Australian per-spectives on confidentiality and social work practice', *British Journal of Social Work*, 36: 91–107.

Swift, P. (2002) *Service Users' Views of Social Workers: A Review of the Literature Undertaken on Behalf of the Department of Health*.

London: University of London, King's College, Institute for Applied Health and Social Policy.

Taylor, C. (2006) 'Narrating significant experience: reflective accounts and the production of (self) knowledge', *British Journal of Social Work*, 36: 189–206.

Taylor, C. and White, S. (2000) *Practicing Reflexivity in Health and Welfare*. Buckingham: Open University Press.

Thomas, N. and O'Kane, C. (1999) 'Children's participation in reviews and planning meetings when they are "looked after" in middle childhood', *Child and Family Social Work*, 4: 221–230.

Thomas, N. and O'Kane, C. (2000) 'Discovering what children think: connections between research and practice', *British Journal of Social Work*, 30 (6): 819–835.

Todd, S. and Jones, S. (2003) '"Mum's the word!": maternal accounts of dealings with the professional world', *Journal of Applied Research in Intellectual Disabilities*, 16 (3): 229–244.

Topss UK Partnership, (2002) *The National Occupational Standards for Social Work*. Leeds: Topss England.

Trevithick, P. (2005) *Social Work Skills*, 2nd edition. Buckingham: Open University Press.

Voice for the Child in Care (2004) *Start with the child, stay with the child: a blueprint for a child-centred approach to children and young people in public care*. London: Voice for the Child in Care, Blueprint Project.

Walsh, T. and Lord, B. (2003) 'Client satisfaction and empowerment through social work intervention', *Social Work in Health Care*, 38 (4): 37–55.

Ward, A. (1990) 'The role of physical contact in childcare', *Children and Society*, 4 (4): 337–351.

Wenger, E. (1998) *Communities of Practice*. Cambridge: Cambridge University Press.

Wilkes, T. (2004) 'The use of vignettes in qualitative research into social work values', *Qualitative Social Work*, 3 (1): 78–87.

Williams, B. (2006) 'Meaningful consent to participate in social research on the part of people under the age of eighteen', *Research Ethics Review*, 2 (1): 19–24.

Younge, G. (2006) *Stranger in a Strange Land*. New York: New Press.

Name Index

Subject Index